THOMAS BEWICK AND HIS PUPILS

" He would often professe that to observe the grasse, herbs, corne, trees, cattle, earth, waters, heavens, any of the Creatures, and to contemplate their Natures, orders, qualities, vertues, uses, etc., was ever to him the greatest mirth, content, and recreation that could be : and this he held to his dying day."

LIFE AND DEATH OF BISHOP ANDREWES, 1650.

THOMAS BEWICK.
(AFTER PORTRAIT BY JAMES RAMSAY.)

Frontispiece.

THOMAS BEWICK

AND HIS PUPILS

BY

AUSTIN DOBSON

WITH NINETY-FIVE ILLUSTRATIONS

LONDON

CHATTO AND WINDUS, PICCADILLY

1884

Detroit: Reissued by Singing Tree Press, Book Tower, 1968

Library of Congress Catalog Card Number 69–17340

TO

W. J. LINTON,

ENGRAVER AND POET,

THE STEADFAST APOSTLE OF BEWICK'S "WHITE LINE,"

THIS BOOK IS DEDICATED.

PREFACE

EXCEPT to explain its appearance, there is little
need of preface to the present volume. It is, for
the most part, a reprint of two articles on Bewick
and his pupils, prepared in 1881-82 for the New
York "Century Magazine." That on Bewick,
when illustrated, was found to be too long for
publication in one number. An entire section
devoted to John Bewick was consequently omitted,
and other retrenchments were effected. In this
reissue, the portions withdrawn are restored; and
such corrections and additions as a writer usually
makes in the case of a paper republished some time
after it was written, have been inserted. The
account of the Pupils, which, when first printed,
was not abridged, has not now been materially
altered. In both cases it would obviously have

been easy to further extend and amplify. But though something might have been gained in substance, more would have been lost in symmetry, while the general result would remain unchanged.

To have written too little on a subject, moreover, is scarcely a fault,—nay, in this particular instance it may almost be claimed as a merit. Few men have suffered as much as Thomas Bewick from that kind of admiration in which enthusiasm plays a far larger part than judgment. Over most of his earlier work, and over all his inferior work, Oblivion, without accusation of blindness, might advantageously " scatter her poppy ;" and the plain-spoken philosopher of Gateshead, who had no desire " to feed the whimsies of the bibliomanists," would have heartily concurred in any such arrangement. What is most durable in Bewick, as it appears to those who prize him judiciously, is Bewick himself,—always provided that Bewick himself is attainable. Since he first restored it in England a hundred years ago, the art of wood-engraving has considerably progressed. As an Engraver pure and simple, many, including some of his pupils, have rivalled him in mechanical dexterity of line and mere manipulative skill. But as an Artist and Naturalist, copying Nature with that loving awe which fears to do her wrong by the slightest deviation from the truth,—as a Humourist and Satirist, criticising life with the clear vision of independent common sense,—his gifts are distinctly " non-transferable." They are at their best in his best work ; and it is on his best work that I have most willingly lingered in these pages, frankly neglecting his less individual efforts. In the words of Chaucer's Man of Law—

> " Me list not of the chaf ne of the stre
> Maken so long a tale, as of the corn."

It remains for me to put on record what obligations I have incurred in my task. To the Editors of the " Century Magazine," who, under great difficulties, spared no pains to illustrate my text effectively, my first and best thanks are due. To my friend Mr. J. W. Barnes of Durham, who has throughout aided and encouraged me in the kindest way, I cannot but feel especially indebted. To Messrs. E. and J. W. Ford of Enfield, to Mr. T. W. U. Robinson of Houghton-le-Spring, to Mr. G. P. Boyce, to Mr. Frederick Locker, Mr. F. Hargrave Hamel, and Mr. J. Waddon Martyn I am grateful for valuable assistance; as also to Messrs. Harper of New York, Messrs. Cassell & Co., and Messrs. Griffith and Farran, by whose courtesy I have been able to increase the number of my illustrations. Lastly, to my English publisher, Mr. Andrew Chatto, who, though my investigations have taught me to differ in some trifling details from the too-little recognised labours of his father, nevertheless placed his father's notes at my disposal; and to Mr. Robert Robinson of Newcastle, who, having himself a long-desired book on Bewick in preparation, did not on that account regard me as a wolf in sheep's clothing, I hereby tender my sincere acknowledgments.

AUSTIN DOBSON.

Porth-y-Felin, Ealing, W.

CONTENTS

CHAPTER I.

CHAPTER II.

CHAPTER III.

CHAPTER IV.

CHAPTER V.

CHAPTER VI.

LIST OF ILLUSTRATIONS

[*₊* *The above illustrations are from (1) copies on the wood, (2) copies by process, and (3) electrotypes from the original blocks. The majority have appeared in the "Century Magazine" and Chatto's "Treatise on Wood-Engraving." The photographs used were taken, under the author's superintendence, by Messrs. Downey of Newcastle.*]

THOMAS BEWICK & HIS PUPILS.

CHAPTER I.

INTRODUCTORY.

DURING the earlier part of the eighteenth century engraving on wood can scarcely be said to have flourished in England. It existed—so much may be admitted—but it existed without recognition or importance. In the useful little "État des Arts en Angleterre," published in 1755 by Rouquet the enameller,—a treatise so catholic in its scope that it includes both cookery and medicine,—there is no reference to the art of wood-engraving. In the "Artist's Assistant," to take another book which might be expected to afford some information, even in the fifth edition of 1788, the subject finds no record, although engraving on metal,

B

etching, mezzotinto-scraping—to say nothing of
"painting on silks, sattins, etc."—are treated with
sufficient detail. Turning from these authorities
to the actual woodcuts of the period, it must be
confessed that the survey is not encouraging.
With the almost solitary exception of the illustrations in Croxall's " Fables of Æsop," to which we
shall hereafter revert, the "wooden engravings"
which decorate books are of the most "stale, flat,
and unprofitable" description. The majority con-
sist of tasteless emblematical ornaments and
"culs-de-lampe," or coarse headpieces, such as
that which Hogarth is said to have designed in
1747 for the "Jacobite's Journal" of Fielding.
Among efforts on a larger scale, the only examples
which deserve mention are the last two plates of
the same artist's "Four Stages of Cruelty," engraved by J. Bell in 1750. These, drawn boldly
on the plank by Hogarth himself, and cut with the
knife in rough effective facsimile, deserve to be
better known, as, besides variations, they possess
an initial vigour of execution which is lost in the
subsequent coppers. It was with a view to bring

the lesson of his sombre designs within the range
of the poorest classes that Hogarth had in this
case selected wood ; but the method was judged
upon trial to be more expensive than metal. Such

SIR BEVIS OF HAMPTON. (FROM A NEWCASTLE CHAP-BOOK OF 1690.)

as it was, nevertheless, the real field of wood-
engraving during the greater part of the eighteenth
century lay among those humbler patrons of art
and literature to whom he desired to appeal. It
was to be found in the rude prints and broad-

sides then to be seen displayed in every farm and
cottage—patriotic records of victories by sea and
land, portraits of persons famous or notorious,

> "—ballads, pasted on the wall,
> Of Chevy Chace, and English Moll,
> Fair Rosamond, and Robin Hood,
> The little Children in the Wood."

Homely mural decorations of this kind, familiar
to Swift in the first years of the century, were, sixty
years later, equally familiar to Goldsmith ; and it
was, doubtless, from some such gallery that honest
Farmer Flamborough or the "blind piper" delighted the simple audience at Dr. Primrose's with
"Johnny Armstrong's Last Good Night," or the
"Cruelty of Barbara Allen." But the execution
of these modest masterpieces was obviously of the
most cheap and rudimentary kind, so that, taking
the woodcut art of the period as a whole, it was
not without some show of justice that Horace
Walpole, preoccupied with the more delicate
effects of chalcography, stigmatised the wood-
blocks of his day as "slovenly stamps."

He was scarcely so fortunate, however, when,
writing in the same place of Papillon's recently

published "Traité historique et pratique de la Gravure en Bois," he went on to doubt if that author would ever, as he wished, "persuade the world to return to wooden cuts." No time, as it chanced, could have been worse chosen for such a prediction, since,—assuming him to have written about 1770,—in the short space of five years later, the "Society of Arts" was offering prizes for engraving in wood, and its list for 1775 contains the names of no less than three persons who received sums of money on this account. The names were those of Thomas Hodgson, William Coleman, and Thomas Bewick. With respect to the first of the trio little needs to be said beyond the fact that he was a Newcastle man, whose signature is found attached to a plate in Hawkins's "History of Music," as well as to certain poorly executed cuts for magazines and ballad-heads, and that he was also a printer and publisher in London. Concerning the second, we learn from the "Transactions" of the Society that he again obtained prizes in 1776 and 1777 for "engraving on wood or type metal," and from Redgrave's "Dictionary" that he died at Duke's Court, Bow Street, December, 1807. To the third belongs the honour of doing what fastidious Mr. Walpole considered so improbable—that is to say, "persuading the world," not all at once perhaps, but gradually, "to return to wooden cuts." It is to the improvements made by Bewick in wood-engraving, and the impulse which it received from his individual genius, that its revival as an art must properly be ascribed—a revival which continues to this day, and which has not yet reached the final phase of its development. But, besides his qualities as a pioneer in his craft, he was an artist and observer of a very rare and exceptional kind, whose best work, in his own line, remains unrivalled. Moreover, he was a man of a singularly attractive northern type, having something both of Hogarth and Franklin in his character, and deserving study as much from his personality as from his talents.

The true record of Bewick's life, like that of most artists, is to be found in his works, which have been voluminously catalogued in Mr. Hugo's "Bewick Collector," 1866-68, and more moder-

ately by Mr. J. G. Bell in 1851. Beyond these,
the chief written sources of information respecting
his career are three in number. The earliest, or
rather the first issued, is a brief memoir contributed in 1831 to the "Transactions of the Natural
History Society of Northumberland, etc.," by Mr.
George C. Atkinson, a gentleman of Newcastle,
who knew him during the last three years of his
life. Next to this comes chapter vii. in Chatto's
"Treatise on Wood-Engraving," the first edition
of which was published by Charles Knight in
1839. John Jackson, the engraver, who supplied
part of the raw material for this book, was a
native of Ovingham, near Newcastle, and for a
short time one of Bewick's pupils. He completed
his apprenticeship under another pupil, William
Harvey. With some reservations, this account
contains many noteworthy biographical particulars,
together with an examination of Bewick's technique. Lastly, there is the memoir composed
by Bewick himself at Tynemouth in November
1822 for his eldest daughter Jane, and published
by her forty years afterwards. This, like the

autobiographical notes of Hogarth which John
Ireland gave to the world, is of the greatest importance, and to Bewick's admirers must always
constitute the standard authority for the points it
covers. Written with a garrulity easily pardon-
able in an author who had almost reached his
seventieth year, but nevertheless strangely reti-
cent regarding his method and his work, it presents a vivid impression of his character and
opinions, and a delightful picture of his youth.

Parentage and early surroundings, according
to Carlyle, are the two great factors in determin-
ing the nature of a man's life ; and by a happy
law of our kind, it is precisely with the recollections of childhood that old age delights most
complacently to linger. The " Memoir " of
Thomas Bewick is no exception to this rule.

CHERRYBURN HOUSE, BEWICK'S BIRTHPLACE,
IN ITS PRESENT CONDITION.
(Part of the Original Structure has been Removed.)   *To face page* 9.

CHAPTER II.

CHERRYBURN HOUSE, Bewick's birthplace, lay upon
the south or right bank of the Tyne, in the parish
of Ovingham, Northumberland, and not very far
from the little village or hamlet of Eltringham.
We say "lay," for the old cottage now only exists
in part, and that part fulfils the homely office of
a "byre" or cowshed, over one door, of which
is the inscription—"Thomas Bewick born here,
August 1753." In the vicinity of this now rises
a larger dwelling, still inhabited by Bewick's
grandnieces. What remains of the older house
formed the central portion of the building shown
in John Bewick's sketch of 1781, printed as a
frontispiece to the "Memoir." Beyond the fact
that the "byre" is still thatched with ling or

heath, and was tenanted, when the writer visited it, by a couple of calm-eyed, comfortable-looking cows, there is nothing about it that calls for especial remark. But the little dean or orchard at the back is still filled with cherry and plum trees, and violets and primroses bloom as of yore beside the now dry bed of the once musical burn which gave the place its name. In Bewick's day there was in this orchard a spring-well under a hawthorn bush, the site of which may yet be traced; while a precipitous little garden to the north presumably remains much as it used to be. From the slope on which the house stands you may look towards the Tyne, still crossed by boat-ferries at Eltringham and Ovingham.[1] Behind you lies Mickley, and away to the left and south formerly stretched the great fell or common, comprising, until it was divided in 1812, some eighteen hundred acres of blossoming "whins" and scented heather, and fine green pasturage, watered by trickling streams. Over the hill to the right are

[1] Since this was first written, the long-desired bridge has been built at Ovingham.

Prudhoe and Wylam; and across the river, also
to the right, rises the square romanesque tower of
Ovingham Church, where Bewick and his brother
John lie buried, and in the parsonage of which—
a pretty old-fashioned stone house with shelving
garden terraces—they went successively to school.
A railway now comes winding from Newcastle
through the Prudhoe meadows, and an embank-
ment runs along the Tyne to Eltringham. But,
in spite of these drawbacks, and the smoky activity of brickworks and collieries hard by, it is not
impossible, on a fresh May morning, with a blue
shower-washed sky overhead, and the young green
triumphing in the shaws and braes, to realise
something of the landscape as it must have looked
more than a hundred years ago, when Thomas
Bewick first saw the light.

His father, John Bewick, was a farmer, who
rented a small land-sale colliery (*i.e.*, a colliery, the
coals of which are sold upon the spot to persons
in the neighbourhood) at Mickley. It is still
worked and held by the present occupants of
Cherryburn. His mother, whose maiden name

was Jane Wilson, came of a Cumberland family.
She was John Bewick's second wife (the first,
Ann Topping, having died childless), and she
bore him eight children, of whom Thomas was
the eldest, and John, born in 1760, the fifth. Another son, William, and five daughters completed
the family. It is with the first-born, however,
that we are chiefly concerned. He appears to
have been sent to school at Mickley when
very young. After the death there of two pre-
ceptors, he was placed, as a day scholar, under
the care of the Reverend Christopher Gregson of
Ovingham, whose housekeeper his mother had
been before her marriage. There is no evidence
that he distinguished himself by any remarkable
diligence, although his after-career shows that he
must have acquired some knowledge of Latin,
and, what is better, of English. On the other
hand, the " Memoir " is full of schoolboy escap-
ades which betoken him to have been a lad of
unusual courage and intractability, earning, in
those days when the rule of the rod was still supreme, no small amount of physical correction from

his father and schoolmaster. Now he is taming a runaway horse by riding it barebacked over the sykes and burns; now frightening oxen into the river for the pleasure of hearing the "delightful dash;" now scampering off naked across the fell with his companions, in imitation of the savages in "Robinson Crusoe." After these misdemeanours, if not locked into the belfry by Mr. Gregson to keep company with the ghosts and bogles, he would steal home, wading the river, and hide himself in the byre-loft until his father's anger should blow over. But, with all this, he was not in any wise bad or vicious. He was truthful and warmhearted, and an appeal to his better feelings was seldom without success. One good quality he also seems to have possessed, not often found in boys. After a gentle reproof from his master's daughter, he never again "plagued" girls in his youth; and he preserved this early respect for women to the last day of his life.

Such not by any means exceptional characteristics are, however, of less moment than those

earlier indications of the tastes which so strongly
coloured his after-life — his love for drawing
and his love of nature.   The former appears
to have been intuitive.   Like Hogarth's, his
"exercises when at school were more remarkable
for the ornaments which adorned them, than for
the exercise itself."   After exhausting the margins
of his books, he had recourse to the gravestones
and the floor of the church porch, which he covered
with rude representations in chalk of devices or
scenes he had met with, and the pastime of the
day at Ovingham was continued in the evening
on the flags and hearth at Cherryburn.   At this
time, he says, "I had never heard of the word
'drawing,' nor did I know of any other paintings
besides the king's arms in the church, and the
signs in Ovingham of the Black Bull, the White
Horse, the Salmon, and the Hounds and Hare.
I always thought I could make a far better hunting
scene than the latter: the others were beyond my
hand."   But although, oddly enough, he makes
no mention of it at this stage of the "Memoir,"
there was another kind of art with which he must

have been minutely acquainted. The house at
Ovingham where the boys kept their "dinner-
poke" during school hours was lavishly orna-

QUEEN ELIZABETH. (FROM A CHAP-BOOK PRINTED BY J. WHITE OF NEWCASTLE.)

mented with those patriotic prints and broad-
sides to which reference has already been made.
Here he might lay to heart the "large and
curious" representation of "His Majesty's Execu-

tion," surmounting the famous "Twelve Good
Rules, found in the Study of King Charles the
First, of Blessed Memory." Or he might devote
himself to the "Battle of Zorndorff," and the
"Sinking of the 'Victory' (Admiral Sir John
Balchen)"; or rejoice over the manly present-
ments of Benbow, and "Tom Brown,[1] the valiant
grenadier." And this was not the only collection. In Mr. Gregson's kitchen was "a remark-
ably good likeness of Captain Coram," the brave
old philanthropist whom Hogarth painted; and
"in cottages everywhere were to be seen the
'Sailor's Farewell' and his 'Happy Return,'
'Youthful Sports,' and the 'Feats of Manhood,'
'The Bold Archers Shooting at a Mark,' 'The
Four Seasons,'" and the like. These popular
knife-cut pictures, considered in connection with

---

[1] The fame of this popular hero is now forgotten; but to-day he
would have earned the Victoria Cross. In 1743, according to
the "Gentleman's Magazine," he was a raw-boned young York-
shireman of eight-and-twenty, not a grenadier, but a private in
Bland's dragoons. At Dettingen he recaptured the standard
single-handed, in which exploit he received five wounds in the
face, head, and neck, two balls in the back, and three through his
hat. Boitard engraved a portrait of him.

the future restorer of wood-engraving, are of greater significance than the ale-house signs.[1]

After he had long scorched his face with his hearthstone designs a friend in compassion furnished him with some drawing paper.

"Here (he says) I had more scope. Pen and ink, and the juice of the brambleberry, made a grand change. These were succeeded by a camel-hair pencil and shells of colours; and, thus supplied, I became completely set up; but of patterns, or drawings, I had none. The beasts and birds, which enlivened the beautiful scenery of woods and wilds surrounding my native hamlet, furnished me with an endless supply of subjects. I now, in

[1] Bewick was not singular in deriving inspiration from these humble sources. "I recollect Sir Joshua Reynolds,—who was present one evening [at Longford's sale] when a drawing was knocked down to his pupil and agent, Mr. Score,—after he had expatiated upon the extraordinary powers of Rembrandt, assuring a gentleman with whom he was conversing, that the effect which pleased him most in all his own pictures was that displayed in the one of Lord Ligonier on horseback, of which there is an engraving by Fisher, the chiaro-'scuro of which he conceived from a rude wood-cut upon a halfpenny ballad, which he purchased from the wall of St. Anne's Church in Princes-Street."— "Nollekens and his Times," 1828, i. 36, 37.

C

the estimation of my rustic neighbours, became
an eminent painter, and the walls of their houses
were ornamented with an abundance of my rude
productions, *at a very cheap rate.* These chiefly
consisted of particular hunting scenes, in which
the portraits of the hunters, the horses, and of
every dog in the pack, were, in their opinion, *as
well as my own*, faithfully delineated. But while
I was proceeding in this way, I was at the same
time deeply engaged in matters nearly allied to
this propensity for drawing; for I early became
acquainted, not only with the history and the
character of the domestic animals, but also with
those which roamed at large."

This brings us to that second taste, the love
of nature. From earliest childhood, when, by the
little window at his bed-head, he had listened to
the flooded burn murmuring through the dean at
the back of the house, or watched, from the byre-
door, the rarer birds—the woodcocks, the snipes,
the redwings, the fieldfares—which in winter
made their unwonted appearance in the frozen
landscape, the sights and sounds of nature had

filled him with delight. To milk the cows, to cut
and "cree" whin-tops for the horses, to carry
straw and oats to the shivering and pastureless
sheep on the fell—these were pleasures not to be
forgotten, and only to be excelled by his favourite
angling, which, with its endless "set gads" and
night lines, its early risings, and late waterside
wadings, occupied the summer months in happy
cares. Then, when the Tyne was flooded and
school a thing impossible,[1] there were the field
sports of the neighbourhood, the "flushing" of
strange fowl by the terriers, the hunting of the
hare and fox, the tracing of the "foumart" (pole-
cat) in the snow, or the baiting of the badger at
midnight. The cruelty of field sports did not at
first present itself to him. Once, however, he
caught a hunted hare in his arms, and was

[1] "During storms and floods, those living on the south side
of the river can neither attend the church, nor, as it sometimes
happens, bring their dead to be buried" (Mackenzie's "Northumberland," 1825, ii. 362). In the last tailpiece of the "Memoir"
a boat is seen waiting at the Eltringham Ferry on a windy day
for a coffin which is being borne down the hill from Cherryburn.
The little pencil sketch which Bewick made for this tailpiece is
still in existence. It belongs to Mr. J. W. Barnes of Durham.

strangely moved by the poor creature's piteous screams of terror. On another occasion the effect was more lasting :—

"The next occurrence of the kind happened with a bird. I had no doubt knocked many down with stones before, but they had escaped being taken. This time, however, the little victim dropped from the tree, and I picked it up. It was alive, and looked me piteously in the face; and, as I thought, could it have spoken, it would have asked me why I had taken away its life. I felt greatly hurt at what I had done, and did not quit it all the afternoon. I turned it over and over, admiring its plumage, its feet, its bill, and every part of it. It was a bullfinch. I did not then know its name, but I was told it was a 'little Matthew Martin.' This was the last bird I killed; but many, indeed, have been since killed on my account."

Different in kind, but connected as closely with the country life, were his interest in, and attraction to, the strange characters of the neighbourhood—characters more common a hundred

years ago than now, when railways and other
facilities for intercourse have done so much
to round off the angles of individuality.   The
winter-night tales of wild exploits in the hunting-
field, and legends of the Border Wars, were a
never-failing source of pleasure.   By the woful
"laments," such as those for the last Earl of
Derwentwater, with whose death it was supposed
prosperity had for ever departed from Tyneside, he was often affected to tears.   Of some of
the cottagers on the fell—poor men whose little
store consisted of a few sheep, a Kyloe cow, or
a flock of geese, and whose sole learning was
derived from Holy Writ, old ballads, and local
histories—he has left portraits which show how
deeply they had impressed him.   One of these was
Will Bewick, a self-taught astronomer, skilled in
stars and planets, upon which he would discourse,
"pointing to them with his large hands, and
eagerly imparting his knowledge . . . with a
strong voice, such as one now seldom hears."
Another was the "village Hampden," Anthony
Liddell, who had formed himself entirely on the

study of the Bible, finding in its precepts reasons
for utter disregard of the game-laws, and exulting
in the jail, to which he was frequently committed,
since he gained the opportunity of reading it
through once more.   Liddell's ordinary appearance—judging from the description of it in the
" Memoir "—must have been almost as remarkable as that of Fielding's " Man of the Hill ":—

    " When full-dressed, he wore a rusty black
coat.   In other respects he was like no other
person.   In what king's reign his hat had been
made was only to be guessed at, but the flipes
[flaps] of it were very large.   His wig was of the
large curled kind, such as was worn about the
period of the revolution.   His waistcoat, or
doublet, was made of the skin of some animal.
His buckskin breeches were black and glossy
with long wear, and of the same antiquated
fashion as the rest of his apparel.   Thus equipt,
and with his fierce look, he made a curious figure
when taken before the justices of the peace; and
this, together with his always—when summoned
before them — undauntedly pleading his own

cause, often afforded them so much amusement that it was difficult for them to keep their gravity."

A third Ovingham worthy was Thomas Forster, called familiarly "Tom Howdy" (midwife) from his mother's occupation, with his stock of secret beehives in the whin bushes; and last, but by no means least, come the swarming old soldiers let loose upon the country at the conclusion of the "Seven Years' War"—old comrades in Napier's and Kingsley's, full of memories of Minden and Lord George Sackville—of James Wolfe and Quebec. Bewick's strong abhorrence of war, which appears so plainly in the later pages of the " Memoir," had not yet been developed, and he listened eagerly to these weatherbeaten campaigners, with their tarnished uniforms and their endless stories about their prowess in the field.

But there comes an end to everything; and the *ineluctabile tempus* arrived at length when a calling must be chosen for the stout boy of fourteen. His taste for drawing determined his apprenticeship to a Newcastle engraver, and he quitted Cherryburn to serve his time with Mr.

Ralph Beilby of that town. The pang of separation was a grievous one.

"I liked my master" (he says); "I liked the business; but to part from the country, and to leave all its beauties behind me, with which I had been all my life charmed in an extreme degree,—and in a way I cannot describe,—I can only say my heart was like to break; and, as we passed away, I inwardly bade farewell to the whinny wilds, to Mickley bank, to the Stob-cross hill, to the water-banks, the woods, and to particular trees, and even to the large, hollow old elm,[1] which had lain perhaps for centuries past, on the haugh near the ford we were about to pass, and which had sheltered the salmon-fishers, while at work there, from many a bitter blast."

These things would be remembered afterwards in the busy city; and though, for a long period, the link with the country was not wholly severed, it is doubtless to those yearning recollections that we owe the rural element in Bewick's work which is its most abiding charm.

[1] This old tree—a note tells us—was swept away in the great flood of November, 1771, to which reference is made at p. 109.

OVINGHAM PARSONAGE.

CHAPTER III.

LOOKING down upon the Tyne from the pleasant parsonage garden at Ovingham, with the round-arched door and dial, and the bright flowerbeds in shadow, it is easy to understand how keenly the boy must have felt the change. Over the broken water at the ferry the swallows are wheeling and turning, while from the other side a rustic group hails the ferryman. Higher up, a man, with raised knees, rides his horse through the river at the ford; a pony and cart come after. Below the ferry an angler is wading mid-deep: on the opposite bank another is throwing a fly. At his back two tiny figures of school-children climb the steep hill to Master's Close. From the tall trees at Eltringham on the right comes the

cry of the cuckoo : on the left the rooks are
cawing in the great rookery at Prudhoe Castle,
the ancient seat of the Umfravilles. There is no
other sound but the rippling flow of the river to
Newcastle and the sea.

But the Newcastle to which it flows to-day is
a far different place from the Newcastle to which
Bewick came in October 1767. One might then,
as now, stand by the famous church of St.
Nicholas, with its fairylike turrets and vanes
and crocketted pinnacles, but the grand High
Level Bridge which Robert Stephenson flung
across the steep ravine between Newcastle and
Gateshead was yet a thing undreamed of. The
keep of the old Norman castle which gave the
town its name, black with age and smoke, still
fronts it at the northern end ; but the spectator
may seek in vain for the frowning and gloomy
gates which stretched across the main streets
from Westgate to Pilgrim Street, or the pleasant
gardens and orchards which everywhere inter-
sected the city, and shut in the stately mansions
and antique houses with carved enrichments,

where dwelt its merchant princes.[1]   The red-brick
shop of Bewick's new master stood near Amen
Corner, and looked into St. Nicholas's Churchyard.   It was distinguishable by two fantastic
wooden spouts, and existed until very lately ; but
a towering building in the modern taste now occu-
pies its site.   Bewick boarded with Mr. Beilby,
and, after the fashion of those days, attended him
to divine service twice every Sunday (probably
carrying the prayer-book),[2] groomed his brother's
horse, and made himself generally useful, not

[1] Some of these expressions are borrowed from a pleasantly-
written little pamphlet by Mr. Robert Robinson, of Pilgrim Street,
issued in 1876 with his reprint of Bewick's " Waiting for Death."

[2] The London apprentices, if we may trust Foote, had somewhat departed from the " beneficial and cleanly way " of life
which still prevailed in the provinces :—

SIR WILLIAM. . . . What, old boy, times are chang'd since the date
of thy indentures; when the sleek, crop-ear'd 'prentice us'd to dangle after
his mistress, with the great gilt Bible under his arm, to St. Bride's, on a
Sunday ; bring home the text, repeat the divisions of the discourse, dine at
twelve, and regale, upon a gaudy day, with buns and beer at Islington, or
Mile-End.

R. WEALTHY. Wonderfully facetious !

SIR WILLIAM. Our modern lads are of a different metal.   They have
their gaming clubs in the garden, their little lodgings, the snug depositories
of their rusty swords, and occasional bag-wigs ; their horses for the turf;
ay, and their commissions of bankruptcy too, before they are well out of
their time.

THE MINOR, 1760, Act i.

omitting, doubtless, to abstain carefully from the
over-abundant Tyne salmon which (as per indent-
ure) the apprentice of the period was not obliged
to eat more than twice a week.

For some time after entering the business
he was employed in copying "Copeland's Ornaments" (Copeland's "New Book of Ornaments,"
1746, or Lock and Copeland's do., 1752, both of
which were in possession of his family), and
"this," he says, "was the only kind of drawing
upon which I ever had a lesson given to me from
any one." So far as the discipline of the hand
is concerned, the statement is no doubt strictly
accurate; but that other education of the sight,
which Hogarth defined as the early habit "of
retaining in his mind's eye, without coldly copying it on the spot, whatever he intended to imi-
tate," had probably been active for many years
previously. Beilby's work was of a most multi-
farious character. Pipe moulds, bottle moulds,
brass clock-faces, coffin-plates, stamps, seals, bill-
heads, ciphers and crests for the silversmiths—
nothing seems to have come amiss; and the

coarser kinds of engraving which fell to the share
of the young apprentice made his hands as hard
and large as a blacksmith's.   According to the
" Memoir," the first "jobs" on which he was employed were etching sword-blades, and blocking
out the wood about the lines on diagrams (to
be finished subsequently by his master) for the
" Ladies' Diary," a popular almanac which dated
as far back as 1704, and which was edited for
many years by Charles Hutton, then a Newcastle
schoolmaster, and later the celebrated Dr. Hutton
of Woolwich.   It was for Hutton also that he did
what in the catalogues figures as his earliest production, namely the diagrams to a " Treatise on
Mensuration."   This book, which long enjoyed
a great reputation, made its *début* in fifty six-
penny numbers (!), and was issued in 1770 as
a portentous quarto volume.   One of the cuts,
often referred to with exaggerated interest,
contains a representation of the tower of St.
Nicholas's Church, afterwards a frequent feature
in Bewick's designs.   Considerable ingenuity appears to have been shown by him in the execution

of these diagrams; and he is said to have devised
a double-pointed graver, so successful in its oper-
ations, that the completion of the work, which had
been begun by Beilby himself, was transferred to
him at Hutton's request.   About the same time

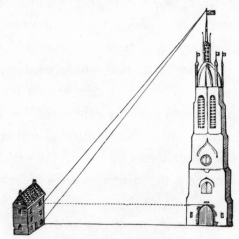

ST. NICHOLAS'S CHURCH.   (FROM HUTTON'S "MENSURATION," 1770.)

he designed and engraved a billhead for the
" George and Dragon " Inn, and (according to
Mr. Atkinson) another for the " Cock," a famous
old hostelry at the Head of the Side.   These performances, though of the rudest character, were
exceedingly popular ; and commissions for work

on wood, which had hitherto been little done in Beilby's shop, began to multiply. Numerous orders for cuts for children's books were received, chiefly from Thomas Saint, a printer and publisher of Newcastle, who had succeeded John White, once famous for his stories and for the old ballads which were sung about the streets on market days. With exception of the Hutton diagrams, the first efforts of Bewick in the way of book-illustration would seem to have been the " new invented Horn Book" and the " New Lottery Book of Birds and Beasts," 1771.

Much caution must, however, be exercised in speaking of these *juvenilia*, which seem to have been unknown to Mr. Atkinson, and are not mentioned in the " Descriptive and Critical Catalogue of Works illustrated by Thomas and John Bewick," published by John Gray Bell in 1851. Specimens of blocks from both of them are given in Mr. Edwin Pearson's reprint of the " Select Fables" of 1784. In the same conjectural category must be placed the " Child's Tutor ; or, Entertaining Preceptor," 1772, the cuts of which

were said by a well-known Bewick collector, Mr.
W. Garret, to have been engraved by Bewick "in
the first year of his apprenticeship, though he
was afterwards ashamed to own them." Next
comes the "Moral Instructions of a Father to his
Son," etc., 1772, at the end of which was a number
of "Select Fables," with thirty-three small illustrations, concerning which we have the express
assurance given by Miss Jane Bewick to Mr.
Pearson in January 1867, that they were the work
of her father. Mr. Pearson also gives examples
of these, which are more interesting than remarkable. The only other work to which, for the present, it is needful to refer, is the "Youth's Instructive and Entertaining Story Teller," published by Saint in 1774. Of this Bewick himself
speaks in the "Memoir," which places its authen-
ticity beyond a question. We do not, however,
propose to linger over these elementary efforts.
They were the tentative essays of an artist who
neither knew his own strength, nor foresaw the
resources of the vehicle he was employing; and
who, when his talents were matured and his voca-

tion found, might well be excused if he declined to be over-communicative respecting work which he had long excelled. Indeed, he excelled it in a marked manner before the termination of his apprenticeship. Among the wood blocks upon which he was busily engaged during the latter part of that period were some intended for an edition of " Gay's Fables." Of five of these Mr. Beilby thought so well that he submitted them to the Society of Arts in London, from whom, as already stated, they received the recognition of a premium of seven guineas, which Bewick at once transferred to his mother.

" Gay's Fables," however, were not published until 1779, and long before that date Bewick had quitted Mr. Beilby's shop. During the time of his bondage, his character and habits became definitely formed. Having fallen into ill-health through over-application and the reading which was almost his sole amusement, the precepts of a sensible Newcastle physician and notability, Dr. Bailes, who seems to have been a kind of local Abernethy, made him turn his attention to questions of diet and exercise. He began to study the regimen of the famous Venetian centenarian, Lewis Cornaro, together with the recommendations as to occasional days of abstinence given, but probably not observed, by the great Mr. Joseph Addison.[1] He thought nothing, he tells us, of setting out, after seven in the evening, to walk to Cherryburn, a distance of more than eleven miles, to see his parents, for whom he maintained the warmest affection, and never failed to visit periodically. These long walks, he adds, were chiefly occupied by the devising of plans for his conduct in life. But it may well be that the insensible education through the senses during his solitary expeditions was of even more importance than the forming of resolves, however praiseworthy, to pay ready money, and never to live beyond his means.

He did not always continue to be an inmate

[1] A little copy of Cornaro's " Sure and Certain Methods of attaining a Long and Healthful Life," etc., dated 1727, and roughly rebound in sheep, is in the possession of the present writer. It once belonged to Robert Elliot Bewick, and is possibly the identical copy which was his father's companion when wandering on the Town Moor, or in the Elswick fields.

of Mr. Beilby's house in the churchyard. After
due time he went to lodge with an aunt, and
subsequently with a flax-dresser and bird-fancier
named Hatfield. Here he had an opportunity of
becoming acquainted with very varied company.
Those of the trade who visited his landlord in his
capacity of flax-dresser were a worthless and dissolute race; but (as might be conjectured) to the
tales of the bird-catchers and bird-dealers who
resorted to the house he listened with the greatest
interest. Among the acquaintances whom he
made about this time was Thomas Spence, the
philanthropist, who was already actively promul-
gating the doctrine, still preached in our own day,
that property in land is everyone's right; and at
"his school on the Quayside" (spelled "Key-
side"), elaborating his new alphabet and phonetic
system of orthography. For some of his types
Bewick cut the steel punches; but, though he
believed him to be sincere and honest, he does not
appear to have unreservedly espoused his prin-
ciples, and his failure to support them on one
occasion at a debating society resulted in a bout

with the cudgels, in which the philosopher behaved so unphilosophically, and even unfairly, that Bewick was obliged to give him "a severe beating."

Others of Bewick's associates were better chosen, if they could scarcely be regarded as less peculiar, than the remarkable author of "The Teacher of Common Sense," and "Pigs' Meat; or, Lessons for the People." Foremost of these come the Grays, father and sons. The father, Gilbert Gray, was a bookbinder, and a thoroughly estimable man. He had previously been assistant to Allan Ramsay, after that worthy wigmaker had left off "theeking the outside of the pash in order to line the inside," and was writing the "Gentle Shepherd." When Bewick knew Gray he was advanced in years, and following his trade in Newcastle. He lived in the most primitive way, eating when he was hungry, sleeping when he was drowsy, and spending his money on the publication of little books of the moral and entertaining class (the "Countryman's Treasure," "Multum in Parvo," the "Complete Fabulist," etc.), which he sold to the people who attended the market on Saturdays. On winter evenings his workshop was the resort of a number of young men, to whom his advice and example were of considerable service. In that of his son, William Gray, also a bookbinder, Bewick was enabled to consult volumes which would otherwise have been sealed to him, and often before his own labours had begun for the day he might be found studying the treasures his friend had to bind. But the genius of the family was George Gray, a fruit-painter of considerable local eminence, and a good geologist, chemist, and botanist to boot. In this last capacity he travelled through great part of North America — no common feat in 1787. He is described as extremely eccentric, both in his dress and habits. Moreover, he was a confirmed misogynist, until a serious illness for the moment perverted him to the belief that " man is not born to live alone." Whilst under the influence of this enervating change in his opinions, he married a shoemaker's widow ; but after her death declared that all the riches of Mexico and Peru should not tempt him to repeat the experiment. George

Gray was five years younger than Bewick. It must, therefore, be assumed that in speaking of him at this stage of the "Memoir," Bewick was anticipating an acquaintanceship which belongs to a somewhat later date.

TAILPIECE. (FROM FERGUSON'S "POEMS," 1814.)

CHAPTER IV.

"WANDERJAHRE."

ON the 1st of October 1774, the seven years' apprenticeship expired; and Bewick, after working for a short time with his old master at a guinea a week, returned to Cherryburn, where he remained until 1776. He continued to execute woodcuts and other commissions, chiefly for Thomas Angus, a printer of Newcastle, and occupied his leisure, as of old, with angling and field-sports, growing more and more attached to the country sights and ways. His later recollections dwell lovingly upon the genial Christmas festivities of the gentry and farmers, when the air was filled with old tunes, with the cheery notes of the Northumberland small-pipes,[1] with the buzz

[1] A bagpipe, differing from the Scotch, being smaller, and

of the "foulpleughs" or Morrice-dancers; and he
sighs for the days gone by, when home-brewed
ale was honest malt and hops.   In the summer of
1776 the spirit of wandering seized upon him,
and, sewing three guineas in his waistband, he
made a long pedestrian excursion to Cumberland
and the lake country,—thence to Edinburgh
and Glasgow.   Passing up the beautiful valley of
the Leven from Dumbarton to Loch Lomond,
he paused to puzzle out the inscription on the
monument of Smollett, of whose works he was as
great an admirer as Carlyle, and so wandered
northward to the Highlands.   Here, having made
up his mind not to visit any town or stay at any
inn, he travelled from one farmhouse to another,
meeting everywhere with kindly and simple hos-
pitality, and pursued, at his departure, by the
customary bannocks and scones.   *À propos* of
one of these leave-takings, occurs the only idyllic
passage in the "Memoir" :—

    "On one occasion, I was detained all day and

blown, not with the breath, but by a pair of bellows fixed under
the left arm.—Brockett's "Glossary."

all night at a house of this kind, in listening to
the tunes of a young man of the family who
played well upon the Scottish pipes. I, in turn,
whistled several Tyneside tunes to him; so that
we could hardly get separated. Before my
departure next day, I contrived by stealth to
put some money into the hands of the children.
I had not got far from the house till I was pursued by a beautiful young woman, who accosted
me in 'badish' English, which she must have got
off by heart just before she left the house, the
purport of which was to urge my acceptance of
the usual present. This I wished to refuse; but,
with a face and neck blushed with scarlet, she
pressed it upon me with such sweetness—while I
thought at the same time that she invited me to
return—that (I could not help it) I seized her, and
smacked her lips. She then sprang away from
me, with her bare legs, like a deer, and left me
fixed to the spot, not knowing what to do. I
was particularly struck with her whole handsome
appearance. It was a compound of loveliness,
health, and agility. Her hair, I think, had been

flaxen or light, but was tanned to a pale brown by being exposed to the sun. This was tied behind with a ribbon, and dangled down her back ; and, as she bounded along, it flowed in the air. I had not seen her while I was in the house, and felt grieved because I could not hope ever to see her more."

He left Scotland in a Leith sloop, arriving at Newcastle on the 12th of August 1776. The passage from Leith to Shields was an exceedingly bad one, and it is characteristic of his kindness of heart that during the whole of the time, although worn out for want of sleep, he tended a poor little baby, which had been put into his bunk for security during the utter prostration of its mother.

After remaining long enough in Newcastle to earn the money for his journey, he took a berth in a collier for London, where he arrived in October. In London he had numerous friends. The Gregsons, his old schoolmaster's sons, and distant connections as well, were established there. William Gray, too, was a bookbinder in Chancery Lane ; and there were others besides. He got

work at once from Isaac Taylor, the master of
another Newcastle acquaintance, and also from
the beforementioned Thomas Hodgson, then a
printer and publisher in George Court, Clerken-
well.   Mr. Atkinson also says he worked " with
a person of the name of Cole," of whom, as a
wood-engraver, Chatto could subsequently find
no trace.[1]   It is possible, however, that this is a
mistake for Coleman, the Society of Arts prize-
man, who, as already pointed out, survived until
1807.   Be this as it may, notwithstanding his
facilities for obtaining employment, Bewick soon
began to weary for St. Nicholas's steeple and
" Canny Newcassel."   London had few charms
for him,—it was too huge, too gloomy, too full of
extremes of wealth and poverty.   With many of
his fellow-workmen he was out of sympathy ; they
called him " Scotchman," and he despised them
as cockneys.   The result was, that in spite of the

---

[1] Redgrave, however, mentions two engravers on copper of
this name.   One of them—B. Cole—executed most of the large
plates for Maitland's " London," and copied for the " Grand
Magazine of Magazines," 1759, the curious frontispiece designed
by Pope himself to the " Essay on Man."

remonstrances of his principal patrons, he resolved to return to his northern home, not so much— as Mackenzie in his "History" would have us believe—because he was "disgusted with the vanity, arrogance, and selfishness of the wood engravers in the proud Metropolis," since those objectionable qualities are not confined to any class or town, but because he was hungering for his "fitting environment"—the Tyne-side, the old folks at Cherryburn, and the simple country pleasures that he loved. He told a friend that he would rather enlist than be tied to live in London; and, years after, the feeling was as strong as ever. Writing in April 1803 to one of the Gregsons, he says :

"I wonder how you can think turmoiling yourself to the end of the Chapter, and let the opportunity slip, of contemplating at your ease the beauties of Nature, so bountifully spread out to enlighten, to captivate and to *cheer* the *heart of man*—for my Part, I am still of the same mind that I was in when in London, and that is, I would rather be herding sheep on Mickley bank top than remain in London, although for doing so I was to be made the Premier of England."

Thus, after brief trial, ended Bewick's *Wanderjahre*. He returned to Newcastle, taking up his abode as before at Hatfield's, and accepting such engraving, either on wood, silver, or copper, as came in his way. He had not been long at work on his own account, when propositions were made to him to enter into partnership with his old master, Mr. Beilby. This, by the intermediation of a friend, was brought about, though not without some misgivings on Bewick's part. He took his brother John, then a lad of seventeen, as his apprentice, and the old weekly visits to Cherryburn were resumed in company. For eight years these were continued in all weathers, winter and summer, fair and foul. Often he had to wade a pool at the outset, and sometimes the river at the end. But by this time his constitution was so hardened by temperance and exercise that neither heat nor cold had much effect on him. And the severities of the winter were amply compensated by the delights of the other seasons when the

valley of the Tyne put on all its beauties, and
he could watch the succession of plants and wild
flowers, and the flight of birds and insects.   Then
again, at this period he had the fullest enjoyment
of his sole diversion — fishing, to the praise of
which he has devoted one of his happiest and
most enthusiastic pages :

"Well do I remember mounting the stile
which gave the first peep of the curling or rapid
stream, over the intervening, dewy, daisy-covered
holme—boundered by the early sloe, and the haw-
thorn-blossomed hedge—and hung in succession
with festoons of the wild rose, the tangling wood-
bine, and the bramble, with their bewitching
foliage—and the fairy ground—and the enchant-
ing music of the lark, the blackbird, the throstle,
and the blackcap, rendered soothing and plaintive
by the cooings of the ringdove, which altogether
charmed, but perhaps retarded, the march to the
brink of the scene of action, with its willows, its
alders, or its sallows—where early I commenced
the day's patient campaign.   The pleasing excite-
ments of the angler still follow him, whether he is

engaged in his pursuits amidst scenery such as I have attempted to describe, or on the heathery moor, or by burns guttered out by mountain torrents, and boundered by rocks or gray moss-covered stones, which form the rapids and the pools in which is concealed his beautiful yellow and spotted prey.   Here, when tired and alone, I used to open my wallet and dine on cold meat and coarse rye bread, with an appetite that made me smile at the trouble people put themselves to in preparing the sumptuous feast; the only music in attendance was perhaps the murmuring burn, the whistling cry of the curlew, the solitary water-ouzel, or the whirring wing of the moor game.   I would, however, recommend to anglers not to go alone; a trio of them is better, and mutual assist-ance is often necessary." [1]

[1] This last piece of advice is at variance with the final words of the first patroness of fishing in England.   "Whanne ye pur-poos to goo on your disportes in fysshyng," says Dame Juliana Berners (if we may still call her so), "ye woll not desyre gretly many persones wyth you, whyche myghte lette you of your game. And thenne ye maye serue God deuowtly in sayenge affectuously youre custumable prayer. . . . And all those that done after this rule shall haue the blessynge of god & saynt Petyr, whyche

In 1785, Bewick's mother, father, and eldest
sister died, and the walks to Cherryburn came to
an end. In the following year he was married to
Miss Isabella Elliot of Ovingham, one of the little
girls whom he had " plagued " in his unregenerate
boyhood. He was then living at the Forth, a large
piece of public ground near St. Mary's Hospital, in
a house which had been previously tenanted by Dr.
Hutton, part of whose furniture he had purchased.
It was a "fine, low, old-fashioned" building, situated
in what was afterwards known as Circus Lane (so
probably called from the Amphitheatre erected in
the Forth in 1789), and having a long garden
extending almost to the old Town Wall. From
the windows could be seen the ancient semi-cir-
cular bastions known respectively as Gunner or
Gunnerton Tower and West Spital Tower. Of
Gunnerton Tower there is a little picture in one
of the tailpieces to the " Water Birds," and it
is stated that the adventurous youngster who is
scaling its crumbling sides for jackdaws' nests (in

he theym graunte that wyth his precyous blood vs boughte."—
" The Treatyse of Fysshynge wyth an Angle," Pickering's reprint,
1827, p. 40.

the original sketch he has a bright blue coat) is
intended for Bewick himself. West Spital Tower
had been turned into a dwelling-place, where lived
Mr. Beilby and his family. Bewick was an enthusiastic florist, and especially fond of roses. His
garden, as may be guessed, was a great pleasure
to him; and his picturesque red nightcap, en-
circled by the fumes of his contemplative "church-
warden," might often be detected there on Sunday
afternoons.

TAILPIECE. (FROM FERGUSON'S "POEMS," 1814.

E

CHAPTER V.

"GAY'S FABLES," "SELECT FABLES."

FOR many years after the termination of his apprenticeship, Bewick appears, by his own account, to have been fully employed upon the business of the firm, which consisted chiefly of work for silversmiths, watchmakers, and hard-waremen. Much time was also occupied in seal-cutting; but engraving on wood, as is clear from the small number of acknowledged works between 1774 and 1784, must have been the exception rather than the rule of his trade. Among the books belonging to this date is the well-known "Tommy Trip's History of Beasts and Birds," published by Saint in 1779, which, owing to the fact that it is supposed by Atkinson and others to have prompted the "Quadrupeds" and "Birds," has acquired a factitious reputation with collectors. A limited reprint of this was issued by Mr. Pearson in 1867. It is also probable that Bewick executed a few cuts when in London for Hodgson's "Hieroglyphick Bible," which appeared about this time. This again was a book for children with emblematical cuts of select scenes from the Old and New Testaments. Then there is the "Lilliputian Magazine," the letterpress of which Mr. Pearson boldly attributes to Goldsmith. It was published in 1783 by T. Carnan, the successor of Goldsmith's friend Newbery, but had probably been printed earlier by Saint at Newcastle.[1] The two volumes, however, with which we are most concerned during this period are the "Fables by

[1] The following passage respecting "Tommy Trip" and Goldsmith is taken from one of Miss Jane Bewick's letters to Mr. Edward Ford, of Old Park, Enfield, and has been kindly communicated to us by that gentleman :—

"My sister lately drew my attention to the passage you quote in the 'Vicar of Wakefield' (Goldsmith's charming little puff [in chapter xviii.] of his children's books, published by Newbery), 'Tommy Trip and his Dog Jowler,' and 'Woglog the Giant.' Well do I remember the little book—amongst many charming Newberys still preserved, that treasure has disappeared. We had it before we could read. The book contained many cuts of animals (a crocodile among the rest), the descriptions of which

the late Mr. Gay" of 1779, and the "Select
Fables" of 1784, both of which were printed and
published by Saint. In these, rather than the
foregoing, interesting as those are from the collector's point of view, Bewick's work began its true
development, and they alone constitute his real
beginnings.

The illustrations to "Gay's Fables," it has
been stated, had been begun during Bewick's
apprenticeship. In advertising them Saint referred to the "finely engraved frontispiece" and
"very curious cuts," some of which had "gained
the premium of the Royal Society [*sic*]." The

were probably compiled by Goldsmith. The cuts must have
been executed while my father was in London.

"I have often heard my father tell that, when he was very
young, a stranger travelling on foot, and dressed in a sky-blue
coat, with immensely large cuffs, called at Cherryburn, where he
had some refreshment. Whilst resting, he conversed with my
grandmother, and when he left she observed to her sister Hannah:
'That is no common person.' The impression made on the
child (Goldsmith was sure to have noticed the little black-eyed
boy) was so strong that the first time he saw a portrait of Goldsmith he felt certain that it was the poet himself who had called
in. One may suppose the fare offered to have been eggs and
bacon with home-brewed birch-wine, which my grandmother used
to make by tapping the birch trees."

"finely engraved frontispiece" was a poor copperplate by Beilby of the monument which Gay's
patrons, the Queensberrys, had erected to him in
Westminster Abbey, and it was manifestly copied
from Scotin's engraving after Gravelot in the Lon-

THE HOUND AND THE HUNTSMAN. (FROM "GAY'S FABLES," 1779.)

don edition of 1738. The "curious cuts" were
sixty-seven in number, not including thirty-three
vignettes. Of the five approved by the "Society of
Arts," the "Old Hound" ("The Hound and the
Huntsman") is the only one which has been identi-
fied. The others, probably executed at different
times between 1773 and 1779, are of very various

merit. Many of them plainly reproduce the compositions of William Kent, Wootton the animal painter, and Gravelot, in the first editions of the two series of "Gay's Fables," issued by Tonson and Knapton in 1727 and 1738 respectively. Whether Bewick made use of these books directly, or followed some intermediate copyist, such as the unknown artist of Strahan's complete edition of 1769, is immaterial. But a comparison of his illustrations with the earlier ones establishes a remarkable relationship, especially in the more allegorical or mythological subjects. In the unpleasant "Universal Apparition," the design is almost exactly similar to that of 1727; the same remark applies, more or less, to the "Miser and Plutus," "Pythagoras and the Countryman," the "Monkey who had seen the World," and others. In all of these, as a rule, Bewick has the advantage in drawing and accessory, although his delineations of nude figures and personifications of any kind are never his happiest work. In the "Farmer's Wife and the Raven," and the "Courtier and Proteus," though still mindful of the earlier plate, he produces something infinitely better.   The former, with its bridge and castle in the background, and the hopeless collapse of "blind Ball" and his rider in front, is one of the best pictures in the book ; and the persuasive man of the world, with his hand, like that of his prototype, on his heart, might have stept from a canvas by Hogarth.   So might the really admirable figure of the bullying and belligerent virago with arms akimbo, in the "Scold and the Parrot." In the "Hare and Many Friends" the arrangement of the first illustrator, Wootton, is almost entirely discarded ; and the gasping, pathetic posture of "Poor honest Puss" appealing vainly to the calf is worthy of a Landseer in little.   Now and then, again, Bewick's knowledge of domestic animals or his keen eye for character overmaster him entirely, and he breaks away from the model altogether.   "The Hound and the Huntsman" is a case in point; it might have been sketched at Cherryburn.[1]   Other examples in this class are

[1] An original pencil sketch for "The Hound and the Huntsman" is in the possession of Mr. Edward Ford, who obtained it from Miss Jane Bewick.

"The Man, the Cat, the Dog, and the Fly," and "The Squire and his Cur." These two are not so much illustrations of Gay as little pictures in *genre*. In one the country gentleman, mottle-faced and condescending, listens with dignity to the tenant, who,

> " . . . . in a bondman's key,
> With 'bated breath, and whispering humbleness,"

addresses his patron ; in the other an old officer, with his hanger and cocked hat on the wall—a true contemporary of Le Fevre and "My Uncle Toby"—is talking to his dog and cat in a room whose conspicuous decoration is a print of a naval engagement. These, as far as we can ascertain, are Bewick's own, and they are of the best.

Generally speaking, the printing of all these cuts, even in the earlier editions (and it is absolutely useless to consult any others), is weak and unskilful. The fine work of the backgrounds is seldom thoroughly made out, and the whole impression is blurred and unequal. Nevertheless, as book illustrations, in detail, composition, and especially in expression, they are far beyond any-

thing of the kind that had appeared before, except a few cuts by Bewick himself, to which we
now come.

The other book of importance belonging to
this period is the "Select Fables," published by
Saint in 1784. Its full title is "Select Fables,
in Three Parts. Part I. Fables extracted from
Dodsley's. Part II. Fables with Reflections, in
Prose and Verse. Part III. Fables in Verse.
To which are prefixed, The Life of Æsop; and
an Essay upon Fable. A New Edition, improved. Newcastle: Printed by and for T. Saint.
MDCCLXXXIV." In reference to the words "a new
edition, improved," it will be remembered that, as
already stated on p. 32, Saint had in 1772 issued a
small number of "Select Fables" at the end of the
"Moral Instructions of a Father to his Son," etc.,
the cuts to which were said by Miss Bewick to
have been her father's early work. Of this book
Saint brought out a third edition in 1775; and in
1776 he issued a volume of "Select Fables" only,
of which the "Select Fables" of 1784 is obviously
an elaboration. In fact, the title-pages are almost

textually identical, and the same emblematic
vignette is used for both. The volume of 1776
contains one hundred and fourteen small and
poorly executed cuts, and, at the end of the book,
in illustration of the "Fables in Verse (Part III.),"
are fourteen larger and better cuts, with borders.
The smaller cuts, which include those in the
" Moral Instructions," are, we must perforce
decide, by Bewick. The " Treatise on Wood-
Engraving," indeed, speaking of them in a foot-
note (p. 480, edition 1861), says that " Bewick
always denied that any of them were of his engraving." But, even if we had not Miss Bewick's
authority for believing to the contrary, this is
contradicted by the book itself, for no less than
thirteen of the remaining fourteen cuts with borders
are reproduced in the " Select Fables" of 1784,
the illustrations of which are attributed to Bewick
by common consent. It must therefore be conjectured either that Mr. Chatto misunderstood
Bewick or his informant, or that he had not seen
the very rare edition of 1776, which is now before
us. So again, when Mr. J. G. Bell and Mr.

Hugo speak of the "miserable" illustrations of
the earlier edition of the "Select Fables," it must
be concluded that they were not aware that the
edition of 1776 contained a number of the cuts
afterwards printed in the volume of 1784. The
smaller cuts are indifferent enough ; but the fourteen at the end are quite as good as those in the
"Gay's Fables" published in 1779. It would be
tedious to carry this purely bibliographical dis-
cussion farther; but it so far disposes of one
troublesome passage in the "Memoir," which
states that, during his apprenticeship, Bewick
was at work on the "Select Fables." That,
before 1774, he could have been working at the
edition published in 1784 is improbable ; but
when it is explained that he prepared cuts for the
edition of 1776, the words are no longer difficult
to understand.

Most of the illustrations to the "Select Fables"
of 1784 show a very marked advance upon those
to the "Gay." The animals are better drawn,
and the backgrounds and details more carefully
studied. But the greatest improvement is in the

grouping. This, and the arrangement of black and white, are much more skilful and effective than before. As before, however, Bewick seems to have been contented to take an earlier work for the basis of his designs. There can be but little doubt that the one used was the " Fables of Æsop and Others," translated by Samuel Croxall, D.D., sometime Archdeacon of Hereford. This was one of the most popular books of the eighteenth century. First published by Tonson and Watts in 1722, by 1798 there had been no fewer than sixteen editions. In the " Treatise on Wood-Engraving" the author, discussing this collection at some length, appears to think that the illustrator, who deserves a better fame than he has obtained, was a certain E. Kirkall, to whose book-decorations Pope refers in the "Dunciad"—

" In flow'rs and pearls by bounteous Kirkall dress'd " ;

and who, we may add, enjoys the unenviable distinction of having pirated Hogarth's " Harlot's Progress" before that ill-used artist could issue his own prints. Mr. Chatto also points out that many of Croxall's cuts are apparently reversed

copies of copperplates by Sebastian le Clerc in an
edition of "Æsop," published circa 1694.[1]   It is
possible, however, that the real originals may be
looked for nearer home, since comparison of the
Archdeacon's book with the fine old folio "Æsop"

THE FOX AND THE GOAT.   (FROM SEBASTIAN LE CLERC.)

of Francis Barlow, once " eminent in this line of
Fowl and Beasts," and sold (as the engraved
title-page has it) "at his House, The Golden

[1] We have failed to trace this edition.   Jombert's " Catalogue
Raisonné " of le Clerc's works, 1774, i. 281, does indeed refer
to a set of " 22 petits ovales en travers, sans le titre," in illustration of "Æsop's Fables," but goes on to say expressly : "Cette
suite . . . n'a servi à aucun livre."

Eagle, In New Street, near Shoo-Lane, 1665,"
reveals unmistakable affinities between the two,
though it would perhaps be hazardous to declare
that Croxall's designer copied from Barlow rather
than le Clerc. A point of more material interest

THE VIPER AND THE FILE. (FROM CROXALL'S "FABLES," 1722.)

in connection with Croxall is, whether the cuts
were engraved on wood or type-metal. Bewick, in
the "Introduction" to the later "Æsop" of 1818,
affirms the latter, though other authorities think
it unlikely. Between experts it is dangerous to
decide; but we are disposed to agree with Bewick.
After carefully comparing Croxall's first edition of

1722 with his tenth of 1775, we are able to affirm
de visu that the cuts in the latter, as impressions,
are to the full as good as those in the former.
It would have been difficult, we imagine, in the
early days of the revival of woodcut-printing to

THE VIPER AND THE FILE.   (FROM "SELECT FABLES," 1784.)

show many books of which this could be said, and
we conceive it to be greatly in favour of the theory
that the illustrations to Croxall were from engravings "on metal in the manner of wood." That
this was practised is plain from the fact that the
Society of Arts twice gave premiums to William
Coleman for work of this very class.

To return, however, to Bewick and the "Select
Fables" of 1784. It is scarcely necessary to show
in detail in what the likeness to Croxall consists,
as a couple of examples will amply suffice—the cuts
to the "Viper and the File," and the "Young Man

THE YOUNG MAN AND THE SWALLOW. (FROM CROXALL'S "FABLES," 1722.)

and the Swallow." In the former Bewick has
closely followed the earlier design. But the advantage in execution, in black and white, and in
the superior fidelity of the accessories (*e.g.* the
vice) is wholly on his side. So are the improvements in the relative proportions of the different
objects—the viper of the old illustrator for size

might be a youthful boa constrictor. In the
"Young Man and the Swallow" the deviations
are more apparent than the resemblances, and
little of similarity remains but in the attitude
of the hero. The swallow which, in Croxall,

THE YOUNG MAN AND THE SWALLOW. (FROM "SELECT FABLES," 1784.)

assumes the proportions of a barn-door fowl is,
in Bewick, reduced to reasonable dimensions.
Croxall's spendthrift has literally denuded himself; but he of Bewick's drawing, like a civilised
eighteenth-century rake, has only pawned his
linen. Again, beyond the bare-boughed tree
there is no particular suggestion of winter in

F

Croxall; but in Bewick there is obvious ice and
men sliding upon it, while he has given to the
chief figure a look of nose-nipped and shivering
dilapidation which is wholly absent from its model.
These specimens will show how Bewick dealt
with Croxall when he employed him as a basis.
But, as in the case of the "Gay," there are numerous instances where the invention appears to be
wholly his own, and they are generally the
happiest in the book. Take, for example, the
charming little pictures of the "Wolf and the
Lamb," and the "Proud Frog." Or (to choose
some fables not given in Croxall at all) let us turn
to the "Hounds in Couples," the "Beggar and his
Dog," the "Collier and the Fuller." This last,
especially, is a little *chef-d'œuvre* for truth to
nature. The fuller with his bare legs and beater;
the grimy but not unfriendly collier; the linen
bleaching in long rows in the field behind, and
the colliery works on the hill,—to say nothing of
St. Nicholas's spire in the distance,—all these go
to make up a whole not afterwards excelled by
any of the famous tailpieces. Bewick was familiar

with fullers and colliers, with frogs and dogs, and
what he knew intimately he could draw as no
other man could.

In contrasting Bewick's work with that of the
unknown illustrator of Croxall, and the illustrators
of "Gay's Fables," it can scarcely be necessary

THE EAGLE AND THE CROW. (FROM "SELECT FABLES," 1784.)

to point out that we have no sort of intention to
depreciate Bewick's gifts. That he should have
chosen to work in a measure upon the lines of
some of his predecessors is no reproach to him,
since it is only what many greater men have done
before and after him. " It was not the subject
treated" (as Mr. Lowell says finely of Chaucer
in similar case), "but himself, that was the new

thing." He brought to his designs an individuality, a personal character, which is wholly
absent from his prototypes. His reproductions
of animal life prove conclusively how infinitely
superior in apprehension and insight he was to
Barlow and Wootton, professed and popular
animal painters; while as a delineator of character
and humanity we must seek for his equals in ranks
far higher than that of the charlatan William
Kent. But his illustrations to these fables are
interesting in another way. Those who admire
his draughtsmanship have often asked themselves
how he obtained his proficiency as an artist, for
he certainly did not acquire it from " Copelands'
Ornaments." The only answer given by his family
is that "he used to go out and look at things, and
then come home and draw them."[1] That is to
say, he shared the instinctive perceptive faculty

[1] Bewick's daughters, it may be observed, could give but
little definite information respecting the growth of their father's
genius. Their appreciation of it was affectionate rather than
enlightened ; and they appear to have shrunk from admitting
that he could possibly be indebted to anything but his own inborn
creative power, even where natural objects were concerned.

and eye-memory of Hogarth and Wilkie ; but
this scarcely explains his skill in combining and
arranging his material.   If, however, we bear in
mind that he spent so much of his early life in
adapting, correcting, and modernising the designs
of others, it requires no further argument to show
that he studied in a school of composition which,
whatever its restrictions, was yet of a practical
and serviceable kind.

TAILPIECE.   (FROM FERGUSON'S "POEMS," 1814.)

CHAPTER VI.

JOHN BEWICK.

In designing and engraving the foregoing "Gay's
Fables" (1779) and "Select Fables" (1784), it
has been asserted that Bewick was assisted by his
younger brother John, whom he had taken as an
apprentice in 1777. In the "Advertisement" to
an edition of the "Select Fables," published by
Emerson Charnley of Newcastle in 1820,—an
edition which, if it was not issued with Thomas
Bewick's approval, was obviously issued within
his knowledge,—this statement as regards those
fables in particular is definitely made; and it is
repeated by Bell and Chatto respecting both col-
lections. Hugo also follows it with regard to
the "Select Fables." On the other hand Atkinson's sketch is completely silent as to such a colla-

boration, although, by his own showing, the writer
was acquainted with Charnley's book ; and there
is no reference to it in the short account of John
Bewick which appears in Mackenzie's "History
of Northumberland." In Bewick's "Memoir,"
too, where some acknowledgment to this effect,
if needful, might have been reasonably expected,
there is not a word upon the subject. As a matter
of fact, it is difficult to understand what material
aid the younger brother could have rendered to
the elder in the "Gay's Fables," seeing that he
was only in the second year of his apprenticeship
when it was first published. To the "Select
Fables," the argument of inexperience does not
apply with equal force ; but it may be noted that
John Bewick's work, for many years subsequent
to 1784, will not, either in draughtsmanship or
engraving, sustain a comparison with the illustrations in that volume. Moreover—though this is
of minor importance—for at least two years previous to its appearance, John Bewick had been
resident in London. Upon the evidence of the
books themselves—we may add—it is impossible

to arrive at a decision ; but the existence of this
moot question may be our excuse for introducing
here some brief account of John Bewick's less
doubtful works.

According to the "Memoir of Thomas Bewick,"
John Bewick continued in his apprenticeship for
about five years, when his brother "gave him his
liberty," and he left Newcastle for London. Here
he found immediate and active, though not lucra-
tive employment, chiefly on blocks for children's
books. Hugo's "Catalogue" gives us the titles
of some of these—"The Children's Miscellany"
(by Day of "Sandford and Merton" fame) ; the
"Honours of the Table ; or, Rules for Behaviour
during Meals ;" the "History of a Schoolboy ;"
the "New Robinson Crusoe," and so forth,—
publications which no doubt were highly popular
with the "little Masters and Misses" in frill-collars
and mob-caps, who resorted to Mr. Stockdale's in
Piccadilly, or Mr. Newbery's at the "Bible and
Sun" in St. Paul's Churchyard. The date of the
"Robinson Crusoe" is 1788, and many of its cuts
are signed. But the first work of real importance

attributed to John Bewick is an edition of Gay's
"Fables," printed in the same year for J. Buck-
land and others, in which, with minor variations
and some exceptions, the earlier designs of Thomas
Bewick are followed.   This book affords an
opportunity of comparing the brothers on similar

ROBIN HOOD AND MAID MARIAN.   (FROM RITSON'S "ROBIN HOOD," 1795.)

ground, and the superiority of the elder is incon-
testable.   Next to this comes a volume which has
usually been placed first, the "Emblems of Mortality," published by T. Hodgson in 1789.   This
is a copy of the famous "Icones" or "Imagines
Mortis" of Holbein, from the Latin edition issued
at Lyons in 1547 by Jehan Frellon, "Soubz l'escu de

Coloigne," with a few supplementary cuts from the
French edition of 1562. Hugo associates Thomas
Bewick with John in this work; and we have
certainly seen an edition which has both names on
the title-page. The early writers, nevertheless,

ROBIN HOOD AND LITTLE JOHN. BY T. BEWICK. (FROM RITSON'S "ROBIN HOOD," 1795.)

assign it to John Bewick alone; and this view is,
in our opinion, confirmed by the following extract
from a letter of Thomas to John, published
by Mr. Hancock of Newcastle in the "Natural
History Transactions of Northumberland," etc.,
for 1877. "I am much pleased," says Thomas
Bewick, "with the Cuts for 'Death's Dance,' and

wish much to have the book when it is done.   I
am surprized that you would undertake to do
them for 6s. each.   You have been spending
your time and grinding out your eyes to little
purpose indeed.   I would not have done them for
a farthing less than double that sum. . . . I am
glad to find that you have begun on your own
bottom, and I would earnestly recommend you to
establish your character by taking uncommon pains
with what work you do."   The quotation seems
to indicate that John Bewick had set up on his
own account in November 1787, the date of the
letter to which the above is an answer.   It gives
an idea besides of the prices paid for wood-engraving both in London and Newcastle, which, as may
be seen, were on anything but a liberal scale.[1]

Even in these days of Amand-Durand facsimiles, the " Emblems of Mortality " is a praiseworthy memento of those marvellous woodcuts

---

[1] Sometimes, too, they do not seem to have been paid at all.
At a sale a few years ago there was sold an autograph letter of
Thomas Bewick to Sir Richard Phillips of the "Million of Facts,"
in which reference was made to a bill for " Botanical Cuts " that
had been outstanding for eleven years !

which, as we are now taught to believe, the obscure
Hans Lutzelburger engraved after Holbein's designs.   In detail, John Bewick's copies vary considerably from the originals ; and, in one instance,
that of the "Creation," where the earlier illustrator
has represented the first person of the Trinity in

THE DEATH OF ROBIN HOOD.   (FROM RITSON'S "ROBIN HOOD," 1795.)

a papal tiara, his imitator, by editorial desire, has
substituted a design of his own.   But the spirit of
the old cuts is almost always fairly preserved, and,
considering the hasty and ill-paid character of the
work, its general fidelity to Holbein is remarkable.
After "Death's Dance" come a little group of
books, chiefly intended for the education of children.

Of these it is impossible to give any detailed
account, nor is it needful, since they have all a
strong family resemblance.   The two first, " Proverbs Exemplified" (1790) and the "Progress of
Man and Society" (1791) are due to the excellent
but wearisome Dr. Trusler, who, with the best

THE RECOMPENSE OF VIRTUE.   (FROM THE " BLOSSOMS OF MORALITY," 1796.)

opportunities, has the honour of being the worst
of Hogarth commentators.   The former book is
sufficiently described by its title ; the latter is a
kind of modern version of the old Latin and high
Dutch "Orbis Pictus" of Comenius, published at
Amsterdam in 1657.   Both of these books are
undoubtedly illustrated by John Bewick alone,

whose name is given in the preface to the "Proverbs." Besides these there are the "Looking
Glass for the Mind" (1792), the charming little
"Tales for Youth" (1794), "Robin Hood" (1795),
and the "Blossoms of Morality" (1796).

The appearance of the "Blossoms of Morality"
was for some time delayed in consequence of the
illness of the artist, and long before it was published, John Bewick was sleeping in Ovingham
Churchyard. His health had been early impaired
by the close confinement of the Metropolis, and
though a visit to Cherryburn seems to have
partially restored him, he was finally obliged
to return to his native air in the summer of
1795, and shortly afterwards died of consump-
tion. In the year of his death was published
a sumptuous edition of the "Poems of Goldsmith and Parnell," due to the enterprise of that
energetic Novocastrian, William Bulmer, of the
"Shakespeare Printing Office," whom his contem-
poraries fondly likened to the Bodonis and Elze-
virs of old ; and the preface proudly sets forth the
excellences of its type, its printing, its Whatman

THE HERMIT. *To face page 79.*

BY T. BEWICK, AFTER JOHN JOHNSON. (FROM "POEMS BY GOLDSMITH AND PARNELL," 1795.)

paper, and its embellishments.[1]   To this book
John Bewick contributed one cut, drawn and engraved by him in illustration of the well-known
passage in the " Deserted Village " respecting the
old watercress gatherer.   He is also understood
to have designed two of the vignettes and one

ROBIN HOOD AND LITTLE JOHN.   (FROM RITSON'S " ROBIN HOOD," 1795.)

of the tailpieces.   During the last months of his
life he was engaged in making sketches on the

---

[1] George III. is said to have declined to believe that the cuts
were engraved on wood, and to have requested to be allowed to
assure himself of the fact by inspecting the original blocks.   But
in these early days of woodcut art, even a George might be
forgiven for not being a connoisseur.   One of the best of the
tailpieces represents His Majesty hunting the stag at Windsor.

block for the "Fabliaux" of Le Grand, translated by Way (1796); and for an edition of Somervile's "Chase," issued by Bulmer in the same year. These were chiefly engraved by Thomas Bewick, who, he says in the "Memoir," completed the drawings for the "Chase" after his brother's death. "The last thing (he adds sorrowfully) that I could do for him was putting up a stone to his memory at the west end of Ovingham Church, where I hope, when my 'glass is run out,' to be laid down beside him."

As is generally the case with those who die young, it is somewhat difficult to speak of John Bewick's merits as an artist and engraver. Much of his work bears evident signs of haste, as well as of an invention which was far in advance of his powers of execution. In the earlier books this is especially noticeable. He had plainly a keen eye for character, and considerable skill in catching strongly - marked expression. In the "Proverbs Exemplified," many of the little groups, though rudely rendered, are excellently "felt," and might easily be elaborated into striking studies. It is

not unnatural, perhaps, that Dr. Trusler should
compare his illustrator to Hogarth ; but in such
designs as " All is not Gold that Glitters," and
" Scald not your Lips with Another Man's Pot-
tage," the comparison is not wholly untenable.
His animals, too, are often admirable—witness the

DOMESTIC SCENE.　BY J. BEWICK.　(SOURCE UNKNOWN.)

popular prowling cat in the " Tales for Youth,"
the hunting scenes in the "Chase" (*e.g.* the "Huntsman and Hounds," the "Home of the Otter"), and
many of the vignettes in the children's books,[1]
while he shared with his brother, though in a far

---

[1] A large proportion of these, however, are mere adaptations
of Thomas Bewick's work.

G

less degree, the art of contriving effective back-grounds of rock-work and foliage. One distinctive quality he seems to have possessed, which is not to be found in Thomas Bewick, the quality of grace—a grace artificial indeed, as was much of the

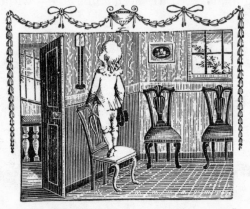

LITTLE ANTHONY.   (FROM THE "LOOKING-GLASS FOR THE MIND," 1792.)

grace of the eighteenth century, yet not without its charm. Whether he caught this from Stothard and the novel illustrators of the period we know not; but there are many examples of it in his work, notably in his treatment of children. Take, for instance, the trio of scholars in the "Progress of Man," who, with their hands on their hearts,

THE SAD HISTORIAN. *To face page* 83.
DRAWN AND ENGRAVED BY JOHN BEWICK.
(FROM "POEMS BY GOLDSMITH AND PARNELL," 1795.)

are "making a leg" to their nightcapped and dressing-gowned preceptor. Or take again the charming picture in the "Looking Glass for the Mind," of the anxious little fellow who is standing on a chair to look at the barometer. As an engraver John Bewick does not in any way equal his brother. His manner is flatter, more conventional, less happy in the distribution of its light and shade. In his later work, however, he improved greatly in this respect, as may be seen by reference to the "Tales for Youth," which contain some of his best engraving, and to the watercress gatherer of the "Deserted Village."

Only one portrait of John Bewick is known to exist, and that is a crayon by George Gray, now in the Newcastle Natural History Society's Museum. Personally he seems to have been a young man of considerable wit and vivacity, and very popular with his associates — a popularity, if we may judge from certain passages in the "Memoir," not without its peril in the eyes of his graver elder brother. " He would not, as he called it, be dictated to by me; but this I persisted in till it made us often quarrel, which was distressing to me, for my regard for him was too deeply rooted ever to think of suffering him to tread in the paths which led to ruin, without endeavouring to prevent it. To the latest day of his life, he repented of having turned a deaf ear to my advice ; and as bitterly and sincerely did he acknowledge the slighted obligations he owed me. He *rued ;* and that is as painful a word as any in the English language." Something in this, no doubt, must be allowed for the Spartan austerity of the disciple of Lewis Cornaro, and it is not probable that poor John Bewick's errors went farther than a certain smartness in costume, and occasional convivial excesses.

At the time of his death he was engaged upon the block of Cherryburn, afterwards used as a frontispiece to the "Memoir." He did not live to complete it ; and it was eventually finished by Thomas Bewick. The original sketch, probably made much earlier, together with his punch-ladle and glass, some water-colour drawings, and other relics, is carefully preserved at the old home by his grandnieces, who still speak affectionately of their "Uncle John's" talents and amiability. At the recent Bewick sale another memento of him came under the hammer. This was a walking-stick, containing a hautboy, with which (as per

LEONORA AND ADOLPHUS. (FROM THE "LOOKING-GLASS FOR THE MIND," 1792.)

catalogue) he is said to have " amused himself in his summer-evening strolls about Hornsey and the banks of the Thames." In the last months of his life, it should be added, he alternated engraving with teaching, being employed as drawing-master at the "Hornsey Academy," then kept by a Mr. Nathaniel Norton. Two or three unfinished

sketches made by him at this time—one of which
shows his pony and his lodgings—are included
in the Bewick bequest to the British Museum.
Another, dated 1795, the year of his death, has
a touch of pathos.   It represents his "intended
house" on the water bank at Eltringham.

TAILPIECE.   (FROM RITSON'S "ROBIN HOOD," 1795.)

CHAPTER VII.

FROM the work of Thomas Bewick previous to
1785, and more especially from the two volumes
of " Fables," it is evident that he is most successful in depicting those phases of animal life with
which he was familiar, or in making such selection as his genius prompted of the characteristics,
whimsical or pathetic, of the humanity about him.

> " That is best which lieth nearest,
> Shape from that thy work of art,"

never received more striking confirmation than at
Bewick's hands. " Hercules and Jupiter," " Time
and Fortune,"—figures in which the allegorists of
the day would have delighted,—become under his
pencil mere lumbering and futile unrealities, ill at
ease in their nakedness, and not to be credited under

any system of theology. But set him down to draw you a group of startled hares, a hungry beggar watched by an equally hungry dog, a boy stung by a nettle, or a brace of snarling hounds — "*impares formas atque animos*"—tugging at the unequal yoke, and he will straightway construct you a little picture—spirited, vivid, irreproachable in its literal fidelity—to which you will turn again and again as to the authentic record of something within your own experience, which you seem to have forgotten, but of which you are glad to be reminded once more. To such an artist, so truthful, so dependent upon nature, so unimaginative (in a certain sense 'of the word), the realising of other men's ideas would be a difficult and uncongenial task. But suppose him to find a field outside these conditions, in which he is free to exercise his abilities in a fashion most pleasant to himself, it will follow, almost as a matter of course, that he will produce his best work. This, in effect, appears to have been the case with Bewick. He found his fitting field in the " Quadrupeds " and " Birds," and rose at once to his highest level.

To face page 89.

THE CHILLINGHAM BULL.

(Reduced Copy from Original Block of 1789. Size of Original Block, 5¼ × 7¾ inches.)

The "Quadrupeds" were begun soon after the publication of the "Select Fables." But while working at them, and before they were published, Bewick produced the large block known as the "Chillingham Bull," one of those famous wild cattle of the old Caledonian breed, now nearly extinct, which Landseer has painted, and Scott has celebrated in the ballad of "Cadyow Castle"—

> " Through the huge oaks of Evandale,
>   Whose limbs a thousand years have worn,
> What sullen roar comes down the gale,
>   And drowns the hunter's pealing horn ?
>
> Mightiest of all the beasts of chase,
>   That roam in woody Caledon,
> Crashing the forest in his race,
>   The Mountain Bull comes thundering on."

The engraving was a commission undertaken in the beginning of 1789 for Marmaduke Tunstall of Wycliffe, a local naturalist and collector ; and in the "Memoir" Bewick has described some of the obstacles he met with in getting near his restless model. " I could make no drawing (he says) of the bull, while he, along with the rest of the herd, was wheeling about, and then fronting us, in the manner described in the 'History of Quadrupeds' (1824, p. 39). I was therefore obliged to endeavour to see one which had been conquered by his rival, and driven to seek shelter alone, in the quarryholes or in the woods ; and in order to get a good look at one of this description, I was under the necessity of creeping on my hands and knees, to leeward, and out of his sight ; and I thus got my sketch or memorandum, from which I made my drawing on the wood. I was sorry my figure was made from one before he was furnished with his curled or shaggy neck and mane."

It is said that Bewick considered this block to be his masterpiece ; and it is certain that the bull with its dark ears and muzzle, its black-tipped horns, its sensitive nostril, and milkwhite hide, is an exceedingly handsome beast. It steps out lightly from a little glade, and halts with its head turned distrustfully toward the spectator, the thin foam threading from its jaws. Its hair and hoofs are excellently given ; but in these days the background and accessories, though minutely careful

and conscientious, would probably be regarded
as stiff and conventional.   When engraved it was
doubtless Bewick's best and most ambitious effort ;
but there are animals and birds in his subsequent
works with which it can scarcely be compared.
An accident, however, has had the effect of giving
the impressions of this block an abnormal value
with collectors—the value of extreme rarity.   After
a few copies had been struck off on parchment and
paper, the block was thoughtlessly laid on a place
where the rays of the sun fell so directly upon it
that it split ; and notwithstanding several attempts
to reunite it, it was never possible to take an
impression which did not betray indications of the
fatal injury.   The sums given for copies taken
before the mishap, without the name and date,
and especially for those on parchment, of which
there appear to have been six,[1] are consequently

[1] There is considerable doubt about the exact number, which
is one of the *cruces* of the Bewick collector. The subject is
exhaustively discussed in Mr. D. C. Thomson's " Life and
Works of Thomas Bewick," 1882, ch. xiii. We may take this
opportunity of adding that much information, not to be found
elsewhere, is contained in Mr. Thomson's attractive volume.

exceptional.   Fifty guineas was paid at one period
of its career for that now in the "Townsend Collection" at South Kensington.   Three more of
the parchment copies were sold with the "Hugo
Collection" in 1877.   The original block, also in
Mr. Hugo's possession, has since passed into the
hands of a gentleman of Northumberland.   Before

THE OUNCE.   (FROM THE "QUADRUPEDS," 1790.)

this, it was cleverly wedged in a new frame of gun-
metal, and a limited number of careful impressions
were taken from it on vellum and toned paper
for Mr. Robinson of Pilgrim Street, from whom
copies, we believe, are still to be obtained.

The account given in the "Memoir" of the
"General History of Quadrupeds," like most of
the portions of that book which relate to Bewick's

work, is of an exceedingly meagre character. But he had actually begun it as early as November 1785, for he was engraving the dromedary when he first heard of his father's death. Most of the cuts and vignettes were executed after the day's work was over, and the letterpress was compiled by Mr. Beilby, who was " of a bookish or reading turn," Bewick giving·him what aid he was of his own knowledge able to contribute, " and blotting out, in his manuscript, what was not truth." Such animals as he knew (he says) were drawn " from memory on the wood," others were copied from Buffon, and others again were from specimens in travelling menageries, first sketched from memory and afterwards corrected on the wood from the animals themselves. In a letter to John Bewick, he speaks of the difficulties that beset him. He cannot get a good idea of the wolf, so contradictory are the reports of its appearance, and he is rejoicing in the advent of " a large collection of animals . . . now on its way to the Town."[1]

[1] This may have been Gilbert Pidcock's, of whose well-known menagerie at Exeter 'Change there is a water-colour in the Crace

In 1790 the "General History of Quadrupeds" was published and sold rapidly. A second and a third edition appeared in 1791 and 1792, and it had reached an eighth in 1824. Its limitations are indicated above. The "Bison" and "Hippopotamus" would scarcely, we imagine, excite the admiration of Mr. Zwecker or Mr. Wolf ; but the dogs, the horses, the sheep, the cows, leave little to be desired. Excellent, too, are the "Badger," the "Hedgehog," and the "Ferret." Chatto is also right in the praise which he gives to the "Kyloe Ox," although our special favourites in the book are the "Spanish Pointer" and the staid "Old English Hound." Some of the backgrounds, those to the domestic animals in particular, are of considerable interest, and often most skilfully contrived to give full effect to the diversities of fur and hide.

Collection. In 1799 Bewick executed four large coarse cuts for Pidcock, a lion, an elephant, a tiger, and a zebra. His own copies of the first two are in the Newcastle Natural History Society's Museum. Besides these large wood-blocks — it may here be added—he also engraved two minutely-finished copperplates, Hall's "Whitley Large Ox," 1789, and Spearman's "Kyloe Ox," 1790. But he attained no special distinction as a chalcographer.

Admirable, however, as was the volume of "Quadrupeds," it was eclipsed by the two volumes of "British Birds." Here the necessity for depending upon incorrect drawings or doubtful

THE OLD ENGLISH HOUND.   (FROM THE "QUADRUPEDS," 1790.)

reports was reduced to a minimum; and Bewick set out with the determination of "sticking to nature as closely as he could." After much preliminary study of such books on ornithology as came in his way, *e.g.* Albin's "Birds," the old "Histoire de la Nature des Oyseaux" of Pierre

Belon,[1] Ray and Willoughby, Pennant and
Latham, he paid a long visit to Wycliffe, where
he remained for nearly two months diligently
copying the stuffed specimens collected by Mr.
Tunstall. Upon returning to Newcastle to make

THE COMMON BOAR. (FROM THE "QUADRUPEDS," 1790.)

his engravings, he was at some pains to reconcile
the discrepancies between those of his drawings

[1] "Belon's very old book," as Bewick styles it, published "at
the Sign of the Fat Hen" ("In Pingui Gallina"), Paris, 1555, is
still worthy the pursuit of the collector, and contains a "vast" of
quaint information, ornithological and gastronomic. Much of it
is sound and valuable, although some of the stories are of the Sir
John Mandeville type. For instance, he relates that "the pelican,
which builds its nest on the ground, finding its young stung by a
serpent, weeps bitterly, and piercing its own breast, gives its own
blood to cure them"—a variation on the older myth. But he is
beyond his age in other things, for, like Mr. Phil. Robinson of the
"Poets' Birds," he says a good word for the vulture.

which had been actually taken from nature and
those which he had copied from preserved figures.
The result was that in many cases he set aside
what he had done to wait for newly-shot birds,

THE STARLING. (FROM THE "LAND BIRDS," 1797.)

with which he was liberally supplied by a few
enthusiastic friends. Several of the sketches were
from life. The "Corncrake," for example, was
taken from a bird which ran about his own room,
and its excellent attitude was cleverly repro-

H

duced by Richard Wingate, a famous bird-stuffer of Newcastle, in a specimen which is still to be seen in that town. It was probably at this date that Bewick made the majority of the very beautiful water-colour drawings exhibited by the Misses Bewick in London, and so excellently annotated by Mr. F. G. Stephens,[1]—drawings

---

1 " Notes on a Collection of Drawings and Woodcuts by Thomas Bewick, exhibited at the Fine Art Society's Rooms, 1880." We quote one just and appreciative passage :—" The ruling element of Bewick's art, technical and inventive, is sincerity. His extreme simplicity, or, to be more precise, his straightforwardness, is but one of the manifestations of this ever-dominant inspiration. He always drew what he saw, and I think it probable that he never drew, or, what is similar, he never painted, anything he had not seen and thoroughly understood. The fund of knowledge thus secured and displayed,—for it is obvious to me that he made himself understand everything he thought fit to draw,—was employed at all times and with the utmost fidelity. He seems to have had so much reverence for his work, and so much humility in the face of nature, that he became the counterpart of another English master in small, William Hunt, the water-colour painter, who, although one of the first men in the world in that peculiar class, was frequently heard to say, ' I almost tremble when I sit down to paint a flower.' But, so far as design goes, and nothing in art is higher, Bewick far surpassed Hunt in the abundance, as well as in the quality, scope, richness, and depth of his invention." There is no indiscretion in now adding that Miss Bewick's very literal and filially indignant comment upon the above was—" Thomas Bewick trembled none ! "

which revealed unsuspected, because hitherto
unmanifested, abilities as a colourist. This sup-
position as to their production is confirmed by
the fact that the " Roller " and the " Red-Legged
Crow," both of which were at Bond Street, are
plainly copies of the stuffed examples still to be
found in the Museum of the Newcastle " Literary
and Philosophical Society," which purchased the
Wycliffe collection. Beyond the specimens possessed by Bewick's family, examples of his water-
colour work, however, appear to be rare. But
Mr. George D. Leslie, R.A., has a beautiful king-
fisher, the praises of which he has written in that
fresh and unaffected book, " Our River."

The first volume of the " Birds " (Land Birds)
was published in 1797. It contained one hundred and seventeen birds and ninety-one tailpieces. The letterpress was by Mr. Beilby;
but the proof-sheets, which were in the late Mr.
Hugo's collection, show that Bewick's amend-
ments and additions were numerous and important. The second volume (Water Birds) appeared
in 1804. The text to this, with some assistance

from the Rev. Mr. Cotes, of Bedlington, was prepared by Bewick, whose partnership with Beilby
had by this time been dissolved. This volume
contained one hundred and one figures and one
hundred and thirty-nine tailpieces. Large addi-

THE YELLOW HAMMER.   (FROM THE "LAND BIRDS," 1797.)

tions were made to both volumes in the succeeding
issues ; and in the sixth edition of 1826 (the last
published during Bewick's lifetime), the first contained one hundred and fifty-seven figures, the
second one hundred and forty-three, besides fourteen supplementary figures of foreign birds. Other

editions appeared after his death, but the latest
(the eighth) is that put forth by Bewick's son,
R. E. Bewick, in April 1847.   In this, "about

THE SHORT-EARED OWL.   (FROM THE "LAND BIRDS," 1797.)

twenty additional vignettes" were inserted from
.a series intended for a projected "History of
British Fishes," left unfinished by Bewick at his
death; the nomenclature and arrangement of
Temminck were adopted; and a synoptical table

of the classification was added. This table was
the work of Mr. John Hancock, a distinguished
naturalist of Newcastle, to whom we are indebted
for some assistance in preparing these pages.

THE EGRET.   (FROM THE "WATER BIRDS," 1804.)

There is no doubt that the "Birds" are
Bewick's highwater mark. He worked in these
under a conjunction of conditions which was
especially favourable to his realistic genius. In
the first place, he was called upon not to invent
or combine, but simply to copy nature with that
"curious eye" which slurs nothing, striving only

to give its full import and value to the fold of a
feather, the tenderest markings of breast and
back, the most fugitive accidents of attitude and
appearance.   Then, having made his drawing in

THE COMMON SNIPE.   (FROM THE "WATER BIRDS," 1804.)

colour or otherwise, he was not obliged to see it
altered or degraded in its transference to the
wood-block at the hands of another person.
Between his original study and the public he
was his own interpreter.   In confiding his work
to the wood he was able to select or devise the
most effective methods for rendering the nice

varieties of plumage, from the lightest down to
the coarsest quill-feather, to arrange his background so as to detach from it in the most telling

THE TAWNY OWL. (FROM THE "LAND BIRDS," 1797.)

way the fine-shaped, delicate-shaded form of his
model, and to do all this with the greatest economy
of labour, the simplest array of lines.   Finally,
besides being the faithfullest of copyists, and the
most skilful of wood-engravers, he was able to

bring to the representation of " these beautiful and
interesting aërial wanderers of the British Isles "
(as he styles them) a quality greater than either
of these, that unlessoned insight which comes of
loving them, the knowledge that often elevates an
indifferent workman into an artist, and without
which, as may be seen from the efforts of some of
Bewick's followers, the most finished technical
skill and most highly trained trick of observation
produce nothing but an *imago mortis*. These birds
of Bewick,—those especially that he had seen and
studied in their sylvan haunts,—are *alive*. They
swing on boughs, they light on wayside stones ;
they flit rapidly through the air ; they seem almost
to utter their continuous or intermittent cries ;
they are glossy with health and freedom ; they
are alert, bright-eyed, watchful of the unfamiliar
spectator, and ready to dart off if he so much as
stir a finger. And as Bewick saw them, so we see
them, with their fitting background of leaf and
bough, of rock or underwood,—backgrounds that
are often studies in themselves. Behind the
rook his brethren stalk the furrows, disdainful of

the scarecrow, while their black nests blot the
trees beyond; the golden plover stands upon his
marshy heath; the robin and the fieldfare have
each his appropriate snow-clad landscape; the
little petrel skims swiftly in the hollow of a wave.
Not unfrequently the objects in the distance have
a special biographical interest. To the left of the
magpie is one of those worn-out old horses, with
whose sufferings Bewick had so keen a sympathy.
It has apparently broken its neck by falling over
a little cliff, part of the rails of which it has carried
with it in its descent. At the back of the guinea-
hen is the artist himself, seated on a wall; in the
cut of the blackbird is a view of Cherryburn.
Details of this kind lead us insensibly to another
feature of Bewick's books on Natural History, of
which we have not yet spoken,—the numerous
vignettes or tailpieces at the ends of the chapters.
These, says his contemporary Dovaston, were
"always his favourite exercise." "The bird or
figure he did as a task; but was relieved by
working the scenery and background; and after
each figure he flew to the tailpiece with avidity,

for in the inventive faculty his imagination re-
velled." Some extravagance of phrase abated,
this statement may be accepted as showing in
which direction Bewick's artistic inclinations were
strongest; and the wide popularity of these little
pictures is another confirmation of Mr. Matthew
Arnold's dictum about "pleasure in creating."
But they deserve a chapter to themselves.

GRACE BEFORE MEAT.   (FROM THE "WATER BIRDS," 1804.)

CHAPTER VIII.

THE TAILPIECES.

MUCH in these famous tailpieces is of that endur-
ing and universal character which belongs to no
time or place. But the pilgrim from Newcastle
to Prudhoe (the nearest point to Ovingham) is
often reminded on the road that he is in Bewick's
country. Passing out of the Central Railway
Station, with the river Tyne to his left, he sees
the " coal-staiths " and fleets of " keels," and the
closed furnace-doors with the smoke curling from
their crevices, as Bewick saw and drew them.
Farther on, at Wylam, they are rook-shooting,
and there are sea-gulls wheeling above the sandy
reaches. While he is punted across the river
from Prudhoe [1] he himself seems to be taking

[1] Now, of course, he crosses the bridge. The above was
written in 1881.

part in a tailpiece, and the spare boat-stower
stuck in the stones of the little pier, and the long
loops of net which are drying in the sun, help to
strengthen this belief. As he climbs the steep
stairway on the opposite bank and notes the tide-
dragged look of the branches near the water, he
is reminded of the frequent floods, and especially
of that great flood of November 1771, which not
only tore down the arches of the old bridge at
Newcastle, but swept away the humbler boat-
house at Ovingham. In the parsonage gate he
recognises an old friend of the "Select Fables,"
and he looks curiously at the picturesque church-
porch where the farmer's son from Cherryburn
once made his "chalky designs." Crossing the
fields again toward Eltringham Ferry a hundred
aspects of hedge and river-side seem friendly and
familiar. The same ploughman is following the
same team as in the vignette of "Justissima
Tellus"; the same sheep are huddling in the fold,
watched by the same vigilant collie; and when
he has traversed the Tyne again, and finds himself among the quaint north-country stiles and

bickering burns, with the water-wagtail busy
among the stones, and the farm-pigeon dropping
down to drink, the illusion is well-nigh perfect.
If, in addition to these, he comes suddenly upon
a detachment of geese with their cackling leader
at their head, marching solemnly waterward in
Indian file, or is startled by an old horse tearing
hungrily at the green leaves of a young tree, he
has no longer any doubt, and believes every line
and stroke that Bewick ever put to paper.

The rural life, and the scenes among which
Bewick was brought up, naturally play a large
part in this attractive collection. At the beginning of the "Land Birds" is that well-known
picture of a "Farmyard," the drawing for which
was exhibited in the Bond Street collection, and
is an extraordinarily minute study of the subject. A woman winnows grain in front; a man
carries a sack to the barn. Cocks and hens,
ducks, turkeys, and geese, and even those unin-
vited guests, the starlings and sparrows, are
clearly distinguishable in the foreground. A sow
enters the yard with her litter; a dog dozes on

the dunghill. Nailed against the byre-wall are a
magpie, a crow, and a heron; over these is a
swallow's nest, or sparrow-bottle. Pigeons fly

A FARMYARD. (FROM THE "LAND BIRDS," 1797.)

above the ricks against the dark background of
the trees, and there is a flight of fieldfares in the
air. The same microscopic truthfulness is exhibited in a dozen other designs. Now it is a
bent old fellow breaking stones by the roadside,

with his dog watching his coat and flask; or
another gingerly crossing the snow-covered ice
astride a branch for safety; a cow that has broken
through a fence to get to the water, or a girl pump-
ing upon a tramp's feet.   We have mentioned
only the principal figures: these are always set in

POACHERS TRACKING A HARE IN THE SNOW.   (FROM THE "LAND BIRDS," 1797.)

their appropriate landscape, and surrounded with
illustrative accessory.   The man crossing the ice,
for instance, is watched by a dog in the background, who is evidently too wary to follow him.

Next to the pictures of rural life come those
which illustrate the sports of the field.   There
are the cruel greyhounds pressing hard upon the
hare; there are the poachers who track her in

the snow; there are the sportsmen who wade the
river, or cross it upon stilts, or reach perilously to
secure their floating quarry, or fraternise at dinner-
time with their dogs. But it is the angler's craft
which is most richly represented, and Bewick has
drawn a score of pictures of this, his favourite
pastime. He shows us the steady-going old
Waltonian " fettling " his hooks under a bank ; the
drenched fisherman watching his " set gads " in
the shelter of a tree ; the salmon-spearer with his
many-pronged " leister." Then there are the
humours and accidents of the game. There is
the excellent but infirm enthusiast who fishes
from his pony's back while his footman waits
hard by with a landing net ; the angler who is
terrified by a turnip-headed " bogle," and the
angler who has hooked a swallow on the wing ;
the angler who has tumbled into the stream ; the
angler who is taking bait from a dead dog, to the
disgust of a companion, who is prudently holding
his nose. And in all these, the little glimpses of
copse and thicket, of brown pool and wrinkling
water, are enough to make a man wish (if he has

I

forgotten the experiences of Washington Irving!)
to become an angler on the spot; and they seem
to find their most restful expression in the charming vignette to which the artist has affixed the
old Virgilian motto adopted by Shenstone at the
Leasowes—"Flumina amem, sylvasque inglorius."

TAILPIECE TO THE "REINDEER." (FROM THE "QUADRUPEDS," 1791.)

In many of the designs already spoken of,
although they are chiefly concerned with the
accurate representation of natural objects, there
are sly strokes of drollery. This brings us to
a special class in these vignettes, namely, those
which are purely and simply humorous,—little
compositions which would have delighted Hogarth,
and hardly dishonoured his genius. Such are the
bottle-nosed and bewigged coachman on the bob-

tailed coach-horse who is following "little master"
on his pony; the black sweep eating white bread
and butter; the old woman (Bewick is unrivalled
at old women) attacked by geese; the depressed
and Callotesque procession with the dancing dogs
and bear; the blind fiddlers led by a ragged boy
and fiddling without an audience; the old husband

TAILPIECE TO THE "WOODCHAT." (FROM THE "LAND BIRDS," 1797.)

carrying his young wife and child across the river
on his back; the drunken miller, who, on King
George's birthday, has been cupping it "till the
world go round," and now lies helpless on his
back, still feebly beating on the reeling earth.[1]
Many of these deserve a page of commentary.
It would be easy, for example, to write at length

[1] This is said to have been a well-known character, one
Rennoldson, a miller at Jesmond.

upon such a theme as that which appears at page
106 of vol. ii. of the "Birds."[1]   Two tramps have
halted at the gate of a pretty cottage garden,
where the mistress is hanging out the clothes.
They have turned away empty and angry, leaving the gate open, and through this the inmates

TAILPIECE TO THE "COMMON CART-HORSE." (FROM THE "QUADRUPEDS," 1791.)

of the adjoining farmyard are successively making their appearance.   The hens have already
occupied the lawn (and the spotless linen); the
little pigs are entering joyfully upon the forbidden
territory; the old sow follows leisurely at the
back.   Another fertile text for disquisition would
be the incident depicted at page 173 of the same

[1] The references, here and hereafter, are to the first editions.

volume.   A man is trying to ford a river with
his cow, to save the toll.   In mid-stream he has
repented of his temerity, but the cow insists upon
proceeding, while her alarmed master pulls help-
lessly at her tail.[1]   The landscape background in
this case, with its bridge and wintry hills, is
excellent for truth and suggestiveness.

TAILPIECE TO THE "JAY."   (FROM THE "LAND BIRDS," 1797.)

Bewick is particularly fond of the especial
kind of dilemma which is illustrated by the last-
named sketch.   He delights in portraying an

[1] This tailpiece recalls a passage in one of Beauclerk's
letters : " Johnson has been confined for some weeks in the Isle
of Sky ; we hear that he was obliged to swim over to the main-
land, taking hold of a cow's tail.   Be that as it may, Lady Di
(*i.e.* Lady Di Beauclerk) has promised to make a drawing of it."
—Hardy's " Life of Charlemont," 1812, i. p. 345.

incident at that supreme moment when, in classic
poetry, it would be considered needful to call in
the assistance of some convenient and compliant
deity.   This is the case of the embarrassed
horseman who figures as a headpiece to the
" Contents " in vol. ii. of the " Birds."   His

KITE-FLYING.   (FROM THE " WATER BIRDS," 1804.)

horse, aged like his master, has been seized with
an ungovernable fit of passive obstinacy.   The
day is rainy, and there is a high wind.   The rider
has broken his stick and lost his hat; but he is
too much encumbered with his cackling and ex-
cited stock to dare to dismount.   Nothing can
help him but a *deus ex machinâ*, of whom there is

no sign.   Another specimen of this sort is the
admirable vignette at page 9 of the same volume.
The string of a kite has caught in the hat of a
man who is crossing a stream on a pony.   The
boys are unwilling to lose their kite, the man

TAILPIECE TO THE " CURLEW."   (FROM THE " WATER BIRDS," 1804.)

clings to his headgear, and it is impossible to
divine how the matter will end.   Sometimes the
humour of these little pictures reaches a point
which can only be designated sardonic.   In its
minor form this is exemplified by the hulking
blacksmith looking on unmoved at the miserable
dog with the pot tied to its tail.   This, however,

may be simply intended as a satire upon brutality. But there are other examples which are not so easy to explain, and less easy to excuse, since they have a kind of heartlessness about them which almost entirely deprives them of their laughable elements. In this category come the

TAILPIECE TO THE "BABOON." (FROM THE "QUADRUPEDS," 1791.)

blind man, whom the heedless or wanton boy is leading into the deep water, and his fellow, whose hat has blown off as his dog conducts him across a narrow and broken-railed bridge. Now and then, again, this kind of incident rises to tragedy, as in the case of the men who are chasing a mad dog almost into the arms of a feeble old woman round the corner, or the tottering child in the

meadow who is about to pluck at the tail of the
vicious colt. We know of no picture of its size which

TAILPIECE TO THE "WATERCRAKE." (FROM THE "WATER BIRDS," 1804.)

communicates to the spectator such a degree of
compressed suspense as this little masterpiece.

But we must abridge what would otherwise
prove too long a catalogue. No list of ours, indeed, could hope to exhaust the "infinite variety"

TAILPIECE TO THE "MISSEL THRUSH." (FROM THE "LAND BIRDS," 1797.)

of these designs; and to turn over the leaves
again is only to discover how many have been
missed or omitted. The exquisite series of

feathers, and the quaint coast-scenes, with their
queer pudding-stone rocks, deserve more than a
passing mention.   So does the little group of
tailpieces which deal with the picturesque "old
soldiers" of Bewick's youth, two of whom head
the "Introduction" to vol. ii. of the "Birds."   A

TAILPIECE TO THE "SHETLAND SHEEP."   (FROM THE "QUADRUPEDS," 1791.)

chapter, again, might be devoted to those alone
which deal with the pathos of animal life, from
the patient outlines of the two horses seen dimly
in the open field through the mist and driving
rain, to that wonderful vignette in the "Quadrupeds" where the cruel, cowardly dog is tearing at
the worried ewe, whose poor little knock-kneed
lamb looks on with mute and helpless bewilder-

ment—a composition which for sheer pitifulness
is not surpassed by Landseer's " Random Shot."
Then there is the section which may be said to
deal with the *lachrimæ rerum*—the sad contrasts
and mutabilities of things—minute pictorial homi-
lies which must have delighted Thackeray : the

TAILPIECE TO THE " ARCTIC GULL.   (FROM THE "WATER BIRDS," 1804.)

ass rubbing itself against the pillar which cele-
brates the famous victory ; the old man reading
"Vanitas Vanitatum " on the crumbling tomb-
stone ; the beggar taking refuge from the rain by
the grass-grown hearth of the ruined cottage ; the
church on the shore, where the waves are rapidly
effacing the records of the dead.   All these, and
many others, are works of art in the truest sense,

and worthy of a far more extensive study than we can give them here.

So unmistakable, too, is the note of reality in the majority of these tailpieces, that it is impossible not to believe that many of them are records of actual occurrences within the recollection of the artist.   It is, therefore, much to be regretted that the late Miss Jane Bewick never carried out her expressed intention of writing a complete and authoritative commentary upon this text.   From some of her letters to Mr. Edward Ford we have, by the courtesy of that gentleman, been able to glean a few particulars upon this subject, some of which are new.   The child catching at the horse's tail in the "Quadrupeds" is Bewick's younger brother ; the woman rushing over the stile is his grandmother.   The tiny vignette at page 122 of vol. i. of the "Birds" represents Bewick's own hat and stick, — the latter, his constant companion, having belonged to John Bewick.[1]   In another vignette (that of the sports-

---

[1] This must be the "blackthorn, full of knobs, with a silver hoop," which Miss Bewick afterwards gave to William Bewick,

man who has missed the snipe and hit the magpie)
is a portrait of " Witch," a favourite dog of the
family ; and Miss Bewick confirms Chatto's statement that the traveller drinking out of the *flipe* of
his hat (" Birds," i. xxx.) is a portrait of Bewick
himself.   There is another in the sketch of the

BEWICK DRINKING OUT OF HIS HAT.   (FROM THE " LAND BIRDS," 1797.)

snow man (" Birds," vol. i. p. 78), where he is
standing on the stool, and his brother is among
the assistants.   Miss Bewick further identifies

the Darlington portrait-painter, saying, her father "never had
any other stick."   In William Bewick's " Life," by Thomas
Landseer, 1871, ii., there are some interesting references to his
greater namesake.   He had a portrait of him by William Bell,
in the Rembrandt style, with a hat on, which does not seem to
have been known to Hugo.

the strong man wading the water with "Long
Longkin," the hero of an ancient Tyneside
ballad of her youth ; and says that the monument
("Birds," ii. 220) is on one of the Northumbrian
plains,—Millfield.   She also confirms the account
given by Atkinson of the two Ovingham dyers,

TAILPIECE TO THE " RED-LEGGED CROW." (FROM THE "LAND BIRDS," 1797.)

carrying a tub between them, in the later editions
of the " Birds " (1816, *et seq.*), although the name
of one is wrongly reported.   It was not Matthew,
but Robert Carr.   The pair were an extraordinary
contrast ; the master being a most dissolute and
objectionable character ; the man remarkable for
his simplicity, integrity, and industry.   The family

of the former, who was fairly well-to-do, have long disappeared; the latter will go down to posterity as the grandfather of the famous engineer, George Stephenson, whose modest birthplace is still passed by all who take the rail for Prudhoe. Another of Carr's grandsons, Edward Willis, was afterwards apprenticed to Bewick. These are minor details; but they increase our regret that the hand which penned them did not complete a task which no one at this distance of time is likely to undertake with any prospect of success.

Several of the original pencil and water-colour sketches for the tailpieces (we may here take the opportunity of stating) are now in possession of Mr. Edward Ford and Mr. J. W. Ford of Enfield. Some of these are of great beauty. Another member of the family, Mrs. Ford, of Adel Grange, Yorkshire, has the water-colour for the vignette (already referred to) of Gunnerton Tower, which is to be found at p. 109 of the "Birds," vol. ii.

In the preceding notes we have made no reference to a few tailpieces in which the humour, coarse but not vicious, is more nearly in accordance with that of certain Dutch painters than the modern taste would approve. But, to the student of Bewick who calls to mind the manners of eighty years ago, these will present no serious difficulty. Another question less easy to dispose of is, What was the amount of the assistance rendered to Bewick by his pupils in the "Land" and "Water Birds"? With trivial exceptions the figures of the birds in the first editions appear to have been entirely done by himself; but, as regards the tailpieces, the author of the "Treatise on Wood-Engraving" goes so far as to give a specific list (pp. 497-8, ed. 1861) of those which, he alleges, were "either not drawn or not engraved by Bewick"—his information being derived from an unnamed pupil.[1] That more than one hand was employed upon the *engraving* of the tailpieces is manifest from the differences in the style of the cuts themselves; but, as may be imagined, these tardy claims on behalf of the pupils were not very

[1] E. Landells, Nesbit, Edward Willis, and William Harvey were all in London about 1835-40; and with each of these (from information now before the writer), in addition to Jackson, Mr. Chatto seems to have been in direct communication.

favourably received by Bewick's representatives
when the "Treatise on Wood-Engraving" was
first published in 1839. No reference, however,
was made to them in any way when the "Memoir"
was issued in 1862, although, in the previous year,
Mr. H. G. Bohn had put forth a second edition
of the "Treatise," in which they were repeated.
This is clearly to be regretted, as the day has now
passed for deciding upon the truth or falsity of
this equivocal list; and it may well be that the
assistance afforded was unduly exaggerated. At
the same time Bewick had some exceedingly
clever pupils, and it is not at all unlikely that two
of them, Robert Johnson and Luke Clennell, did
really render effective service in the tailpieces of
the "Birds," and especially in the second volume.
That this was so, detracts little or nothing, as it
seems to us, from Bewick's reputation. To whatever extent he availed himself of the aid in question, it would be absurd to overlook the fact that he
was the presiding spirit of the enterprise, that his
pupils worked under his direction and influence,
and that, although a few of them attained to re-

markable technical skill as engravers, there is absolutely no evidence that any of them ever excelled him in his own particular line when working by themselves.   It is, however, only just to add that Johnson, some of whose delicate water-colour drawings are still to be seen in Newcastle, must have possessed talents both as a designer and humourist of a really remarkable order.   His story, as told by Mackenzie, is a sad one.   He was born at Shotley in Northumberland, in 1770, being the son of a joiner and cabinet-maker, who placed him in 1788 with Bewick, under whom he rapidly became proficient in drawing.   His sketches found ready purchasers; and his caricatures, in the Cruikshankian vein, considerable popularity.   Hugo gives the names of two or three of these pictorial pasquinades, which were directed against a Newcastle Tory bookseller, Joseph Whitfield.   Johnson does not appear to have engraved much on wood, although he executed at least one copperplate.   The rest may be told in Mackenzie's words: "About six months after the expiration of his apprenticeship, he was engaged by Messrs.

Morrison, of Perth, to reduce the set of portraits by Jamieson, and was sent to Kenmore, the seat of the Earl of Breadalbane, to copy them for the

MEMORIAL CUT TO ROBERT JOHNSON. (AFTER CHARLTON NESBIT.)

Gallery of Scottish Portraits. He had finished fifteen, and there remained four to copy, when, in his anxiety to complete his task, he would sit, though of a delicate constitution, all day in a

room without fire.   A violent cold was the consequence, which, neglected, increased to a fever.
'It flew to his brain; and, terrible to relate! he
was bound with ropes, beaten, and treated like a
madman.'   This improper treatment was discon-
tinued by the orders of a physician who accidentally
arrived.   By the application of blisters, reason
returned; and poor Johnson died in peace on
October 29, 1796, in the twenty-sixth year of his
age.   His friend and fellow-prentice, Nesbit,
engraved a memorial to his memory; and a stone
was erected in Ovingham Churchyard to record
the early fate of this ingenious and promising
artist."

It is worth noticing that, from the above
account, Johnson's connection with Bewick was
clearly long subsequent to the "Select Fables"
of 1784; and that it had ceased some months
before the publication of the first volume of the
"Birds" in 1797.

BUST OF BEWICK.
By E. H. Baily, R.A., in the Newcastle Literary and
Philosophical Society's Library.   *To face page* 133.

CHAPTER IX.

"ÆSOP'S FABLES," BEWICK'S DEATH.

In 1804, when the second volume of the "Birds" was issued, Bewick was a man of fifty. He had still four-and-twenty years to live. But although he continued to occupy himself actively for the remainder of his life, he never again produced anything to equal the "Select Fables" and the three volumes on Natural History. A large number of books, illustrated or said to be illustrated by him, have been traced out by the indiscriminate enthusiasm of the late Mr. Hugo, whose unwieldy collection was dispersed at Sotheby's in 1877. For the revival of many of these—"honest journeywork in defect of better," as Carlyle would have styled them—we suspect that straightforward Thomas Bewick would scarcely have

thanked him. The only volume of any real importance subsequent to 1804 is the "Fables of Æsop,"
published in 1818. If any books issued in the
interval deserve a passing mention they are
Thomson's "Seasons," 1805, the "Hive," 1806,
Burns's "Poems," 1808, and Ferguson's "Poems,"
1814. But the designs for the Thomson and
Burns were prepared by John Thurston, and in
the case of the latter it is stated by William
Harvey that they were engraved by Bewick's
pupil, Henry White. In the "Hive," again, the
majority of the cuts are by Luke Clennell.

The "Fables of Æsop and Others"[1] seems

---

[1] This must not be confused with the vamped-up volume
issued in 1820 by Emerson Charnley under the title of "Select
Fables; with Cuts, Designed and Engraved by Thomas and
John Bewick and Others [!], previous to the year 1784: Together with a Memoir; and a descriptive Catalogue of the Works
of Messrs. Bewick." Charnley, an enterprising Newcastle publisher, had become possessed of the majority of the blocks to the
"Select Fables" (1784) and "Gay" (1779). To these he added
a number of inferior cuts of early date, done chiefly for Saint, including some by Isaac Nicholson and "others," and he put forth
the whole with the above title as "Vol. i. of Bewick's Works."
The "Memoir" and "Descriptive Catalogue" were prepared by
John Trotter Brockett, author of the "Glossary of North Country
Words, in Use," 1825; and Charlton Nesbit, who engraved an

to have been begun in 1812, after a severe illness, to which reference is made in the " Memoir." Bewick speaks of this book as if it had been a long-contemplated idea. " I could not (he says) . . . help regretting that I had not published a book similar to ' Croxall's Æsop's Fables,' as I had always intended to do " [he seems to forget or ignore the " Select Fables "] ; and he goes on to say that, as soon as he was so far recovered as to be able to sit at the window, he began to " draw designs upon the wood " for the illustrations. In this work he expressly states that he was assisted by his son (R. E. Bewick), and two of his pupils, William Temple and William Harvey. It is probable that the bulk of the engraving fell to the share of these latter. But here, again, we come face to face with another of the unsolved, and to-day insoluble, questions of Bewick biography.

excellent frontispiece-portrait of Bewick, after William Nicholson, repaired and retouched the blocks,—not to their advantage. This volume was produced with little consideration for Bewick's feelings and reputation. Its pretensions are well known to collectors ; but Mr. W. J. Linton has recently exposed them at large in the " Academy " for 22d March 1884.

In the "Treatise on Wood-Engraving" it is alleged
that the majority of the water-colour drawings for
"Bewick's Fables" were made by Robert Johnson
"during his apprenticeship," and they are referred
to in a note as if the writer were speaking *de visu*,

THE FOX AND THE GOAT. (FROM CROXALL'S "FABLES," 1722.)

since their "finish and accuracy" is dilated upon,
and they are compared to "miniature *Paul
Potters.*"[1]   It is, of course, possible that this
should be the case, but it seems at the same time
exceedingly improbable that in preparing a book

[1] This note, we have reason to believe, was written by or for
Mr. Jackson.

in 1812, Bewick should have fallen back for his
designs upon a set of illustrations made some
twenty years before by a young man, who, moreover, had been in his grave since 1796. Unfortu-
nately there is not, to the best of our recollection,

THE FOX AND THE GOAT. (FROM "FABLES OF ÆSOP," 1818.)

a single allusion to Johnson in the whole of the
"Memoir," unless, indeed, it is covered by a
passage in which "the envy and ingratitude of
some of my pupils" are obscurely hinted at. It
is therefore hopeless now to speak with any certainty upon the matter.

As to the book itself, it bears much the same relation to Bewick's earlier work that the performances of a man's decline generally do to the first "sprightly runnings" of his genius. The impulse flags, but the effort is painfully increased. The cuts in "Æsop" are more minute and more studied, less certain of stroke, less sparing of line. The basis of the designs, by whomsoever the majority may be, is avowedly Croxall. In the "Viper and the File," for instance, the composition is larger and more minutely finished; but the viper (and this is an improvement) is on the ground instead of on the bench. In the "Young Man and the Swallow" the artist has reverted, not we think wisely, to the classical prodigal of the earlier book. Some of the tailpieces are good and humorous; but they are not equal to those of the "Quadrupeds" and "Birds." A man with a bundle at his back, whose shadow resembles the devil, appears to give the first hint of the ingenious shadow-pictures of the late C. H. Bennett. "Waiting for Death," at page 338, is one of the many variations of the large block upon which

Bewick was occupied in his last days ; and according to Howitt, the inscription at page 152—" O
God of infinite Wisdom, Truth, Justice, and Mercy,
I thank Thee," was Bewick's favourite form of
prayer.   The headstones at pages 162 and 176
record the dates of the deaths of his father and
mother ; and the final tailpiece is said by Mr.

HEADSTONE TAILPIECES.   (FROM " FABLES OF ÆSOP," 1818.)

Hugo to represent John Bewick's funeral.   In
this case the church represented must be intended
for a reversed copy of the one at Ovingham.   The
little tailpiece to the " Frogs and their King," apart
from its special merit, affords us an opportunity of
citing a thoroughly Ruskinesque passage which is
devoted to it in " Ariadne Florentina," pp. 89, 90.
"In this vignette he [Bewick] strikes definitely at
the degradation of the viler popular mind which

is incapable of being governed, because it cannot understand the nobleness of kingship . . . There is an audience of seven frogs, listening to a speaker, or croaker, in the middle; and Bewick has set himself to show in all, but especially in the speaker, essential frogginess of mind—the marsh temper. He could not have done it half so well in painting as he has done by the abstraction of wood-outline. The characteristic of a manly mind, or body, is to be gentle in temper, and firm in constitution; the contrary essence of a froggy mind and body is to be angular in temper, and flabby in constitution. I have enlarged Bewick's orator-frog for you [this refers to the plate in 'Ariadne'], . . . and I think you will see he is entirely expressed in those essential particulars."

Although the legend at the bottom of this cut is undoubtedly a *facsimile* of Bewick's handwriting, it is, however, most likely that it was engraved by William Harvey, as it is wanting in some of the characteristics of Bewick's manner. A curious receipt is generally to be found bound up with copies of " Æsop's Fables." It is inter-

esting to collectors from the example which it
gives of the signatures of the Bewicks, father and
son, and for the famous thumb-mark, which also
appears at page 175 of vol. i. of the "Birds."
Another noticeable feature of this receipt is a
piece of seaweed, which seems to lie over the
central landscape, and was impressed upon it in
red ink from a copperplate. Finally, it should
be added that the "Preface" to the book, which
deserves some of the praise lavished upon it by
the artist's admirers, was written by Bewick himself, who is also responsible for a few of the
fables, that of the "Ship Dog" being from his
hand. Another, composed for the same purpose,
and entitled "The Alarm," was first published in
the "Memoir" of 1862,—Bewick's printer, Mr.
Walker, having made some objection to it, which
led to its suppression in 1818. There are better
examples of the author's prose, and its chief characteristic is the inordinate length of the "application," which is quite in Croxall's vein. The
illustration, also by Bewick, which represents the
imps of hell setting off "like a whirlwind, amidst

the glare of lightning and the roar of thunder, to take up their abode in the minds of men," is here reproduced from the copy given in the "Treatise on Wood-Engraving."

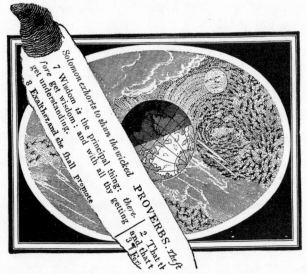

THE ALARM.　(INTENDED FOR "FABLES OF ÆSOP," 1818.)

If we except the account of a brief visit paid to Edinburgh in 1823, when he made for Messrs. Ballantyne and Robertson the only sketch upon the stone (the "Cadger's Trot") which is known to have come from his hand, there is little of

further biographical interest in Bewick's "Memoir."
In the last year of his life he visited London ; but
although the concluding date of the " Memoir " is
1st November 1828, or only a few days before he
died, it contains no reference to that occurrence.
At this time, he was evidently in failing health ;
and it is related that although his friend Mr.
William Bulmer drove him to the Regent's Park,
he declined to alight for the purpose of seeing the
animals. But if the " Memoir" is deficient in
merely personal particulars, it is by no means
deficient in personality, as some dozen further
chapters are exclusively occupied by those reflections with which (as Dovaston informs us with
complacent but comical gravity) "he generally
relieved his powerful mind in the bosom of his
very amiable family." To the ordinary reader
these deliverances would be perhaps a little tedious; but, to the lover of Bewick who cares to
know all about him, they will command the respect with which they are spoken of by Mr.
Ruskin. Most of them are characterised by
strong good sense and natural piety; and in one

or two passages, as, for instance, when he writes on the topics of selection in marriage and the education of children, considerably in advance of his time.

Of what, however, would have interested us most, his method and procedure in his art, he has little definite to tell us. It is possible—as he hints —that, in mistaken modesty, he shrunk from obtruding his opinions. But the two chapters which contain references to this subject must serve as our pretext for recalling briefly the most obvious characteristics of his technique.

In comparing Bewick's method as an engraver with that of the old woodcutters who reproduced the drawings of Durer and Holbein, two marked and well-defined differences become apparent. One of these is a difference in the preparation of the wood and the tool employed. The old woodcutter cut his design with a knife on strips of pear or other wood sawn lengthwise—that is to say, upon the *plank;* Bewick used a graver and worked upon slices of box cut across the grain— that is to say, upon the *end of the wood.* The other difference, of which Bewick is said to be the inventor, consisted in the employment of what is known technically as "white line." In all antecedent woodcutting, the workman had simply cleared away those portions of the block left bare by the design, so that the design remained in relief to be printed from like type. When done skilfully, and with enlightened appreciation of the essential quality — the vigour or delicacy— of the original design, the result obtained in this way is a practical *facsimile*. Clennell's copies of Stothard's pen-and-ink sketches for the Rogers of 1810 are good examples in point. Bewick, however, though of course working sometimes in *facsimile*, generally proceeded in a different fashion. He directed his attention less to the portions of the block which he was to leave than to those he was to remove. Those spaces or lines which in the impression would print black, he left to take care of themselves ; those he chiefly regarded were the spaces and lines which would print white. In other words, whether the design to be copied was brush or pencil—in tint or stroke

L

—he drew it upon the block with his graver in
white line.   This is a bare way of explaining his
modus operandi; but a glance at the background
of some of his cuts, say the "Yellow Hammer" at
p. 100, will make it plainer than any written description.   Again, his gradations of colour were
obtained almost exclusively by the use of single
lines as opposed to cross-hatching; and here
also his mode of approaching his work from
the white rather than the black side was an
advantage.

"I never," he says, speaking of cross-hatching,
"could discover any additional beauty or colour
that the crossed strokes gave to the impression,
beyond the effect produced by plain parallel lines.
This is very apparent when to a certainty the
plain surface of the wood will print as black as
ink and balls can make it, without any further
labour at all; and it may easily be seen that the
thinnest strokes cut upon the plain surface will
throw *some light* on the subject or design : and, if
these strokes are made wider and deeper, it will
receive more light; and if these strokes, again,

are made still wider, or of equal thickness to the
black lines, the colour these produce will be a
grey ; and the more the white strokes are thick-
ened, the nearer will they, in their varied shad-
ings, approach to white, and, if quite taken away,
then a perfect white is obtained."

Another feature of Bewick's method, which
his daughter and editor regarded as "peculiar to
himself," was his habit of "lowering" his blocks
to lighten the impression where necessary. No
doubt he himself hit upon this expedient inde-
pendently, but it seems to have been well known
to some of the earlier engravers, including Croxall's artist. The following passage, from Chapter
XXII. of the " Memoir," refers, *inter alia*, to this
process :—

" The first difficulty I felt, as I proceeded,
was in getting the cuts I had executed printed so
as to look anything like my drawings on the blocks
of wood, nor (*sic*) corresponding to the labour I
had bestowed upon the cutting of the designs.
At that time pressmen were utterly ignorant as to
any proper effect that was to be produced ; or

even, if one of them possessed any notions of excellence beyond the common run of workmen, his materials for working were so defective that he could not execute even what he himself wished to accomplish. The common pelt-balls then in use, so daubed the cut, and blurred and overlapped its edges, that the impression looked disgusting. To remedy this defect I was obliged carefully to shave down the edges round about; and this answered the end I had in view. The next difficulty was worse to surmount, and required a long time to get over it; and that was, to lower down the surface on all the parts I wished to appear pale, so as to give the appearance of the required distance; and this process will always continue to call forth and to exercise the judgment of every wood-engraver, even after he knows what effect his *careful pressman* may be enabled to produce from this his manner of cutting. On this all artists must form their own ideas. I think no exact description can be laid down as a rule for others to go by: they will by practice have to find out this themselves."

It may be added that " no exact description "
of Bewick's method will make a Bewick, any more
than staring at his worn-out graving tools and
eye-glass, which were displayed in the Bond Street
Exhibition, will make an engraver.   In technique,
although the principle of "white line" is still recognised, many improvements have taken place,
and modern wood-engraving has resources never
foreseen by its northern restorer and reviver.
There are, besides, many designers on the block
to-day, compared with whom, by what Mr. Hamer-
ton styles his "tonic arrangement," by his conventional rendering of details, and by his general
treatment of his subject, Bewick must seem an
unlettered amateur.   But his gift as a naturalist
and humourist still remains unaltered,—personal,
unique, incommunicable.   It is this quality which
attracts to him that large majority who are neither
artists nor engravers ; and it is in virtue of this,
and his sincerity and honesty as a man, that his
work will continue to live.

Shortly before his death Bewick retired from
the business in favour of his son, who continued to

BEWICK'S WORKSHOP IN ST. NICHOLAS'S CHURCHYARD, NEWCASTLE,
IN ITS PRESENT CONDITION.

carry it on at the shop in St. Nicholas's Churchyard, where for nearly fifty years his father had
laboured.   It was in the upper room of this house,

we are told—the room which has in our sketch
two windows in the roof—that Bewick preferred
to work in his latter days. The old shop still
presents the same appearance that it did then,
the only difference being that the signboard
bearing the words " Bewick and Son, Engravers,"
is now replaced by a tablet identifying the spot.
On one of the windows, his name, scratched by
a diamond, and the profile of a face, are exhibited with pride by the present occupants. His
residence, after he moved from the Forth, was a
house on the Windmill Hills, Gateshead, which
then commanded a view of the Tyne, but is now
simply No. .19 West Street. Here, after his
retirement, Bewick continued to employ himself
upon the "History of British Fishes," some of the
blocks for which were printed at the end of the
" Memoir ; " while a further selection of the tailpieces, already drawn upon for the " Birds " of
1847, are dispersed in the body of the book.
The last vignette upon which Bewick was engaged was that of the ferry-boat waiting for the
coffin, at page 286 of the " Memoir," and before

referred to in these pages.   But the chief work of
his closing days was a large separate woodcut,
in which it was his aim, by printing from two
or more blocks, to produce something of the
variety of tint and effect obtained in the copperplates of Woollett.   The subject he selected was
a lean-ribbed and worn-out horse, waiting patiently
in the rain for death.   This he intended to serve
as one of those cheap prints for the walls of
cottages which had been familiar to his boyhood,
and he proposed to dedicate it to the "Society for
the Prevention of Cruelty to Animals."   With
some such view he had already, as early as 1785,
drawn up a graphic biography of his broken-down
model.   Besides being an excellent introduction to
his design, it is thoroughly characteristic both of
its author's literary style and his sympathies with
equine misery.   We therefore reproduce it here,
in all the integrity of its italics.

"Waiting for Death.

" In the morning of his days he was handsome
—sleek as a raven, sprightly and spirited, and

was then much caressed and happy. When he grew to perfection in his performances—even on the turf, and afterwards in the chase and in the field—he was equalled by few of his kind. At one time of his life he saved that of his master, whom he bore in safety across the rapid flood, but having, in climbing the opposite rocky shore, received a blemish, it was thought *prudent* to dispose of him, after which he fell into the hands of different masters; but from none of them did he ever eat the bread of idleness, and as he grew in years his cup of misery was still augmented with bitterness.

" It was once his hard lot to fall into the hands of *Skinflint*, a horse-keeper—an authorised wholesale and retail dealer in cruelty—who employed him alternately, but closely, as a hack, both in the chaise and for the saddle; for when the traces and trappings used in the former had peeled the skin from off his breast, shoulders, and sides, he was then, as his back was whole, thought fit for the latter; indeed, his exertions in this *service of unfeeling avarice* and *folly* were great beyond belief. He was always late and early made ready for action—he was never allowed to rest. Even on the Sabbath day, because he could trot well, had a good bottom, and was the best hack in town, and it being a day of pleasure and pastime, he was much sought after by beings *in appearance* something like gentlemen, in whose hands his sufferings were greater than his nature could bear. Has not the compassionate eye beheld him whipped, spurred, and galloped beyond his strength in order to accomplish double the length of the journey that he was engaged to perform, till, by the inward grief expressed in his countenance, he seemed to plead for mercy, one would have thought, most powerfully? But alas! in vain. In the whole load which he bore, as was often the case, not an ounce of humanity could be found; and, his rider being determined to have pennyworths for his money, the ribs of this silent slave, where not a hair had for long been suffered to grow, were still ripped up. He was pushed forward through a stony rivulet, then on hard road against the hill, and having lost a shoe, split his hoof, and being quite spent with hunger and fatigue, he fell, broke his nose and his knees, and was unable to proceed; and becoming greased, spavined, ringboned, blind of an eye, and the skin by repeated friction being worn off all the large prominences of his body, he was judged to be only fit for the dogs. However, one shilling and sixpence beyond the dog-horse price saved his life, and he became the property of a poor dealer and horse doctor.

"It is amazing to think upon the vicissitudes of his life. He had often been burnished up, his teeth defaced by art, peppered under his tail, had been the property of a general, a gentleman, a farmer, a miller, a butcher, a higgler, and a maker of brooms. A hard winter coming on, a want of money and a want of meat obliged his poor owner to turn him out to shift for himself. His former fame and great value are now to him not worth a handful of oats. But his days and nights of misery are now drawing to an end; so that, after having faithfully dedicated the whole of his powers and his time to the service of unfeeling man, he is

at last turned out, unsheltered and unprotected, to
starve of hunger and of cold."

On the Saturday previous to Bewick's death,
which took place, after a few days' illness, on the
8th of November 1828, he had the first block of
the old horse proved.   It was then unfinished, the
head being only partly engraved, but he is said
to have observed to the pressman, upon inspecting the proof, "I wish I was but twenty years
younger!"   Copies of this were struck off in 1832
by R. E. Bewick, with this inscription—"Waiting
for Death : Bewick's Last Work, left unfinished,
and intended to have been completed by a Series
of Impressions from Separate Blocks printed over
each other."   In recent years it has again been
carefully reprinted on parchment and paper for
Mr. Robinson, of Pilgrim Street.

Bewick is buried at the west end of Ovingham Church, lying, as he hoped, beside his brother
John, and near the place of his birth.   In his last
illness his mind wandered repeatedly to the green
fields and brooks of Cherryburn ; and once, on

OVINGHAM CHURCH—BEWICK'S BURIAL-PLACE.   *To face page 156.*

being asked in a waking moment what had occupied his thoughts, he replied, with a faint smile, "that he had been devising subjects for some new tailpieces." The chief features of his personal character will already have been gathered from what has preceded. It is only necessary to add here that he seems to have been a thoroughly upright and honourable man, independent but unassuming, averse to display of all kinds, very methodical, very industrious, devoted to his fireside, his own people, and that particular patch of earth which constituted his world. In such scant glimpses as we get of him in letters and the recollections of friends, it is chiefly under some of these latter aspects. Now he is chatting in his broad speech [1] to the country folk in the market-

---

[1] Bewick, says Mr. Atkinson, spoke grammatically, and with well-chosen and forcible words, but his pronunciation was broad, and marked by all the varied intonation of Northumbrians. He was exceedingly clever in imitating the language of his countrymen, and sometimes scribbled down his recollections of scenes in his early life for the amusement of his friends. Of one of these Mr. Atkinson prints a fragment :—

"'Aehy—Aehy,' kih she, 'yeh may say what yeh leyke, but Ize suer aws reet, aw ken well eneugh when he was bwoarn, fir I meynd aw was up at the Mistrisses suen ee th' moarning, ith th' howl oh

place, or making friends with some vagrant specimen of the brute creation; now throwing off a
sketch at the kitchen table "to please the bairns,"
or working diligently at the "Birds" in the winter
evenings to the cheering sound of his beloved

wounter, when in cam little Jenny runnin—"Muther! Muther!"
sez she, "there cums little Andra Karr, plish-plash throw the
clarts [mire], thockin and blowin, wiv his heels poppin out ov
clogs every step, leyke twe little reed taties—wiv a hare's scut iv
his hat, and the crown of his head and teheyteed hair stanning
up throw't." "Poor fellow" (sez the Mistriss), "aws warn a keahm
hesn't been iv his head this twe months—Andra, Andra!—whats
the mayter? . . . "Wheez there" (sez the Mistriss)? "Wey,
there's our Dehym, an Isbel, and Barbary, and aw so oad Mary,
cummin tappy lappy [full speed] owr the Stob-Cross-Hill, and
Jack Gorfoot galloping by Anty's garth neuk on the oad gray
meer, with Margery the Howdy behint him, fit to brik their
necks!"—"Aehy" (sez the Mistriss), "and I mun away tee—
whares the' fayther, Andra?" "Wey" (sez Andra), "I so him
stannun at th' lown end oh the Byer, wouv his jazey neetcap on,
and his hands iv his kwoat pockets, beayth thrimpt owr his thees—
and glowrin about, but I saw nowse he wis leukin at."—"Sit
down Andra—oh the trow steahyn"—see doon sat Andra, and
weyhpt his nwoase on his kwoat kuff—"meayk heayst lass, an
bring him (poor fella) a shive of butter and breed—cut him a
good lounge, an strenkle a teahyt oh sugar on't," ' " etc.

This passage, with its graphic minuteness of detail, shows that
Bewick could describe as vividly as he could draw, and makes
one regret that more of these studies in dialect have not been
preserved. Meanwhile Margery the Howdie and Jack Gorfoot
survive in one of the tailpieces to the "Land Birds," 1797, p. 157.

Northumberland pipes.   Towards the close of
his life many inquiring, and some distinguished
visitors found their way to the little house in
West Street.   One of these, the American naturalist Audubon, has left a detailed account of his
impressions, which gives a pleasant picture of the
old man and his surroundings.   Audubon reached
Newcastle in the middle of April 1827.   "Bewick
must have heard of my arrival," . . . he says,
"before I had an opportunity of calling upon him,
for he sent me by his son the following note :—' T.
Bewick's compliments to Mr. Audubon, and will
be glad of the honour of his company this day to
tea at six o'clock.'   These few words at once
proved to me the kindness of his nature, and, as
my labours were closed for the day, I accompanied
the son to his father's house. . . .

"At length we reached the dwelling of the
Engraver, and I was at once shown to his workshop.   There I met the old man, who, coming
towards me, welcomed me with a hearty shake of
the hand, and for a moment took off a cotton
night-cap, somewhat soiled by the smoke of the

place. He was a tall stout man, with a large head, and with eyes placed farther apart than those of any man that I have ever seen :—a perfect old Englishman, full of life, although seventy-four years of age, active and prompt in his labours. Presently he proposed showing me the work he was at, and went on with his tools. It was a small vignette, cut on a block of boxwood not more than three by two inches in surface, and represented a dog frightened at night by what he fancied to be living objects, but which were actually roots and branches of trees, rocks, and other objects bearing the semblance of men.[1] This curious piece of art, like all his works, was exquisite, and more than once did I feel strongly tempted to ask a rejected bit, but was prevented by his inviting me upstairs, where, he said, I should soon meet all the best artists of New-castle.

"There I was introduced to the Misses Bewick, amiable and affable ladies, who manifested all anxiety to render my visit agreeable. Among

[1] *Vide* "Memoir," 1862, p. 134.

the visitors I saw a Mr. Goud,[1] and was highly pleased with one of the productions of his pencil, a full-length miniature in oil of Bewick, well drawn, and highly finished.

"The old gentleman and I stuck to each other, he talking of my drawings, I of his woodcuts. Now and then he would take off his cap, and draw up his gray worsted stockings to his nether clothes; but whenever our conversation became animated, the replaced cap was left sticking as if by magic to the hind part of his head, the neglected hose resumed their downward tendency, his fine eyes sparkled, and he delivered his sentiments with a freedom and vivacity which afforded me great pleasure. He said he had heard that my drawings had been exhibited in Liverpool, and felt great anxiety to see some of them, which he proposed to gratify by visiting me early next morning along with his daughters and a few friends. Recollecting at this moment how desir-

[1] This was T. S. Good of Berwick, a too little-known artist, four of whose pictures are in the National Gallery. His portrait of Bewick is now in the Newcastle Natural History Society's Museum.

M

ous my sons, then in Kentucky, were to have a copy of his works on Quadrupeds, I asked him where I could procure one, when he immediately answered 'Here,' and forthwith presented me with a beautiful set.

"The tea-drinking having in due time come to an end, young Bewick, to amuse me, brought a bagpipe of a new construction, called the Durham Pipe, and played some simple Scotch, English, and Irish airs, all sweet and pleasing to my taste. I could scarcely understand how, with his large fingers, he managed to cover each hole separately. The instrument sounded somewhat like a haut-boy, and had none of the shrill warlike notes or booming sound of the military bagpipe of the Scotch Highlanders. The company dispersed at an early hour, and when I parted from Bewick that night, I parted from a friend."

Audubon seems to have visited Bewick on several subsequent occasions, and they separated with mutual regret. He met him but once again after leaving the North. This was when the old man paid his before-mentioned visit to London.

"Our interview was short but agreeable, and when he bade adieu, I was certainly far from thinking that it might be the last.   But so it was, for only a very short time had elapsed when I saw his death announced in the news-papers." [1]

Bewick's family consisted of a son and three daughters, all of whom survived him.   His wife, to whom he was devotedly attached, and with whom (he says) he had spent "a lifetime of un-interrupted happiness," died in February 1826, aged seventy-two.   She seldom figures in the "Memoir," but the following letter, written to her by her husband from Wycliffe in 1791, gives a pleasant idea of their relations.   Had it not been already published in the "Natural History Transactions of Northumberland," etc., there might have been a certain hesitation in giving so domestic a communication to the world. As it is, no one, we think, can read it without being struck by its genuine and simply expressed affection.

[1] "Ornithological Biography," 1835, iii. pp. 300-2, 303.

" Wycliffe, Aug. 8th, 1791.

" My Dear Bell — I never opened a letter
with more anxiety nor read one with more pleasure in my life than I did my Bell's, last week.   To
hear of you being all well gave me the greatest of
pleasures.   How desirous am I to hear of your still
continuing so.—My dear little boy is hardly ever
out of my mind.   I hope the sea will mend him.
If upon my return I find him recovered I think I
shall be frantic with joy. — Indeed if upon my
return I find you all well I shall look upon my
fireside at the Forth like a little Heaven.—I hope
I shall, when I return, but I think it will be about
3 weeks yet before I have that pleasure.   The
young Gentleman has sent Mr. Collier notice that
he will not be at this place till the latter end of
the month.   I have plenty of work before me to
keep me closely employed a much longer time
but I am tired out already and wish it was over.
I have dulled myself with sticking to it so closely.
In short I lose no time in order to get through
with the business.   When you write again tell me
when you will be at the Forth lest I should be at

a loss where to direct to you. Also tell me how
you all are for that is everything with me. Take
care when you return to the Forth lest the beds
should be damp by your long absence. Tell Jane
and Robert that if they behave well I will let
them see a vast of little pictures of Birds when I
come home, and I hope my little Bell will be able
to say more than *dadda* when I see her again.—I
am, with compls. to all, my Bell's loving husband,

THOMAS BEWICK."

Robert Elliot Bewick, the " Robert " of this
letter, and the musician of the Durham pipe, died
unmarried in July 1849, and was buried in Ovingham Churchyard. He seems all his life to have
suffered from ill-health. He copied nature with
great fidelity, and was exceedingly minute and
patient ; but as an engraver he never developed
the latent talent which his father believed him to
possess. Besides some undistinguished assistance
in the " Fables of Æsop," he worked upon the
projected " History of British Fishes." The
" Maigre," a copperplate of which is given at the

end of the " Memoir," bears his signature ; and
in the same book Miss Bewick says that her
brother left behind him "about fifty highly-finished
and accurately-coloured drawings of fishes [1] from
nature, together with a portion of the descriptive
matter relating to the work," which he had pur-
posed to complete, although he never carried out
his intention.   Perhaps, as he once told a gentleman at Newcastle, he was honestly "afeard," and
recognised his incapacity to follow with credit in
his father's footsteps.   Of the three daughters,
the youngest, Elizabeth, died in 1865.   Jane, the
eldest of the family, who edited the "Memoir,"
survived until 7th April 1881, being then ninety-
four.   She is described as a most delightful and
intelligent old lady, full of affectionate veneration
for Thomas Bewick's memory, and abounding in
anecdote respecting his works and ways. [2]   The
only remaining member of the group, Isabella,

[1] These drawings, which form part of the Bewick bequest to
the British Museum, are very beautiful.   Special attention may
be drawn to those of the Gurnard, the Lump Sucker, and the
John Dory.

[2] An extract from one of her letters is printed at pp. 51-2 (note).

lingered for two years longer, and died in June
1883, aged ninety-three.   Not long before her
death she anticipated a bequest which she had
agreed upon with her sister Jane, and transferred to the British Museum a number of water-
colours and woodcuts by her father, his brother
John, and his son.   Some further family relics—
engravings, books, and so forth — were lately
(February 1884) sold at Newcastle by order of
Miss Isabella Bewick's executors, who have also
since presented several valuable portraits, drawings, and prints to the Newcastle Natural History
Society's Museum.[1]   At a future sale,[2] which is
to take place in London, the blocks for the two
volumes of the " Birds," the " Quadrupeds," the
" Fables of Æsop," and the " Memoir," all of
which are said to be in excellent condition, will
come under the hammer.   These represent, or
perhaps we should say include, most of Bewick's
masterpieces.   The remaining blocks of import-

[1] A list of these is to be found at the end of this volume.

[2] This sale took place on the 6th May 1884, the blocks
becoming the property of Messrs. Ward of Newcastle (Miss
Bewick's legatees) for £2350.

ance, the "Select Fables" excepted, belong to
Newcastle collectors,—the majority of them (*i.e.*
those for "Goldsmith's and Parnell's Poems,"
Somervile's "Chase," the "Hive," etc.) being at
present in the hands of Mr. Robert Robinson,
of Pilgrim Street. "Waiting for Death" and the
"Chillingham Bull" are owned by Mr. Thomas
Gow of Cambo; while Mr. T. W. U. Robinson,
of Houghton-le-Spring, has the "Bay Pony" employed in 1801 as the frontispiece to the pamphlet
entitled the "Sportsman's Friend."

There are numerous likenesses of Bewick.
His grandniece, Miss Bewick of Cherryburn, has
a picture of him when young by George Gray.
Then there is the well-known engraving by T. A.
Kidd in 1798, after Miss Kirkley. At West
Street, when Miss Isabella Bewick died, were
two portraits, one being that by Good of Berwick,
which Audubon refers to; the other the original
of the plate issued by Burnet in 1817, after James
Ramsay.[1] At the National Portrait Gallery is

[1] This, together with the Good, the Kirkley, and Plymer's
and Summerfield's miniatures, is now in the Newcastle Natural
History Society's Museum.

BAY PONY.

(From the "Sportsman's Friend," 1801.)

To face page 168.

another half-length by Ramsay, dated 1823, and
purchased by the Trustees in 1871.   A third
and very popular Ramsay is the little full-length
engraved by F. Bacon in 1852, which belongs to
Mr. R. S. Newall of Ferndene, Gateshead.   Mr.
Thomas E. Crawhall, of Condercum, possesses
the water-colour sketch by Nicholson, recently
etched by Leopold Flameng for the Fine Arts
Society.   Another portrait by Nicholson, taken at
Chillingham, and excellently engraved by Charlton
Nesbit, formed the frontispiece to Charnley's
"Select Fables" of 1820.   Besides these there is
a third picture by Nicholson, engraved by T. E.
Ranson in 1816; a miniature, engraved in the
same year by J. Summerfield, after Murphy; and
a miniature by Plymer.   Lastly, there is the bust
by E. H. Baily, R.A., reproduced at page 133,
for which Bewick sat in 1825.   Of this Mr.
Atkinson writes:—"Bailey's (*sic*) bust in the
library of the Literary and Philosophical Society,
of this town [Newcastle], is certainly the best
representation of him, giving the very spirit and
expression of his face, and descending to the

peculiarities of the veins on the temple, the quid
in the lip [Bewick, like Henry Fielding, indulged
in the objectionable habit of 'chewing'], and the
tufts of hair in the ears."   It is said that the artist
wished to drape his model in the classic manner.
The old man, however, with the imperious per-
tinacity of a Cromwell, insisted upon absolute
fidelity, not merely to his coat and ruffled shirt,
but to the "beauty spots," as he called them,
which the smallpox had left upon his face.

BEWICK'S THUMB-MARK.   (FROM THE RECEIPT FOR
"FABLES OF ÆSOP," 1818.)

CHAPTER X.

CHARLTON NESBIT.

WRITING to George Lawford, the publisher, in February 1828, not many months before his death, and speaking of the first series of Northcote's "Fables," Bewick says : "Little did I think, while I was sitting whistling at my workbench,[1] that wood-engraving would be brought so conspicuously forward, and that I should have pupils to take the lead, in that branch of the art, in the great Metropolis ; but old as I am, and tottering on the downhill of life, my ardour is not a bit abated, and I hope those who have succeeded me will pursue that department of engraving still further towards perfection." The accent of satisfaction in these

---

[1] Bewick was an indefatigable whistler, an accomplishment upon which Dovaston dilates with his accustomed grandiloquence.

words is not unnatural, and the improvement of
wood-engraving since they were penned has certainly been greater than Bewick ever anticipated.
Still, it would be a mistake to suppose that its
progress down to 1828, and, indeed, for some years
subsequently, was either very rapid or very remarkable.   Since the publication of the second
volume of the "Birds," in 1804, Bewick himself
had done nothing of importance, with the exception of "Æsop's Fables."   Johnson and John
Bewick had long been dead.   Charlton Nesbit,
the most distinguished of the elder pupils as an
engraver pure and simple, had retired to his
native village, and might practically be regarded
as forgotten.   Luke Clennell, the genius of the
group, had been insane since 1817, and for some
time before had transferred his energies to painting ; while Harvey, Bewick's favourite, was fast
acquiring a reputation as a designer.   A few professed draughtsmen upon wood and half a dozen
engravers seem to have sufficed to the demand.
" The professors of wood-engraving [in Bewick's
time]," says Fairholt, "might be counted by units."

"There were not more than three masters in
London who had sufficient business to employ,
even occasionally, an assistant, and to keep an
apprentice or two," says another writer. If we
turn from these authorities to such treatises as
Landseer's and Craig's "Lectures," the record of
wood-engraving is meagre and apologetic, and it
is easy to see that it was scarcely regarded as a
formidable rival to engraving upon metal. But
in 1828, when Bewick wrote the above letter, its
hour was not the less at hand. The publications
of the recently established "Society for the Dif-
fusion of Useful Knowledge" were already offering it a field which promised to be extensive.
Then in 1832 came the "Penny Magazine" and
the "Saturday Magazine,"[1] which, aided by the

[1] "The art of wood-engraving itself has received an astonishing
impetus from these publications. The engraver, instead of working
merely with his own hands, has been obliged to take five or six
pupils to get through the work" (Mr. Cowper's evidence before
the Select Committee on Arts and Manufactures, 1835). It is
difficult nowadays to understand what a revelation these two
periodicals, with their representations of far countries and foreign
animals, of masterpieces of painting and sculpture, were to middle-
class households fifty years ago. The present writer, though he
can scarcely go back so far, still remembers, with gratitude, that

improvements in stereotype founding, gave an extraordinary impetus to wood-engraving, and the names of Jackson and Branston and Landells, of the two Whympers and Sears, of Bonner, Baxter, Lee, began to be current on men's tongues. As, with the decline of the "Annuals," engraving on steel and copper, for purposes of book illustration, gradually fell into disuse, engraving on wood increased in scope and popularity, and its advance since that time has been continuous and unchecked.

From what has been said above it will be gathered that Bewick had no "school," in the sense in which that word is used by those who inherit the manner and the method of some individual artist. The pupils who quitted him to seek their fortunes in London, either made their way with difficulty or turned to other pursuits, and the real popularisation of wood-engraving did not take place until some years after his death.

to Mr. Fairholt's careful copies of Hogarth's prints in the old "Penny Magazine," he is indebted for an enthusiasm which has never since deserted him.

Still, the careers of his principal apprentices are not wholly without interest; and some brief account of them will not be out of place.

CHARLTON NESBIT, who comes first in order, has this in particular, that, unlike Harvey and Clennell, he lived and died an engraver. As a matter of course he was a draughtsman, but we have found no record that he either painted or designed, at all events to any extent. Accident, moreover, appears to have favoured this limitation of his functions, for the acquirement of sufficient independent means in middle life made it unnecessary for him to follow up very pertinaciously what, about 1810, was apparently a precarious calling, still less to turn to other departments of art for a subsistence. Little is known respecting his life that is unconnected with his work. He was the son of a keelman at Swalwell, a town in Durham, on the banks of the Tyne, and was born in 1775. About 1789 he was apprenticed to Bewick and Beilby; and it is alleged that the bird's nest which figures above the preface to

vol. i. of the " Birds,"[1] as well as the majority of
the vignettes and tailpieces to the " Poems of
Goldsmith and Parnell," were engraved by him
during his pupilage. In 1797 or 8, he executed a

ST. NICHOLAS'S CHURCH. (REDUCED FROM NESBIT'S CUT AFTER JOHNSON.)

block of St. Nicholas's Church, after a water-colour
drawing by Robert Johnson, which is still in the
possession of a Newcastle collector. For this he

---

[1] In the " Treatise on Wood-Engraving " it is stated that he
drew it as well; and we have reason to believe that he himself
supplied this information to Mr. Chatto.

received, not the "gold palette," as stated by
Mackenzie, nor "a medal," as stated by Mr.
Chatto, but the lesser silver palette of the "Society
of Arts," to whom he presented an impression
of the cut, at that time one of the largest ever
engraved, as it measured, with the border, fifteen
inches by twelve. About 1799 he came to London.
In 1802 he obtained a silver medal from the
Society of Arts for "Engravings on Wood," being
then described as "Mr. C. Nesbit, of Fetter Lane."
In 1815 he returned to his native place, where he
lived in retirement, working at rare intervals for
the London and Newcastle booksellers. He
visited London again in 1830, and died at Queen's
Elm, Brompton, in November 1838.

The two principal designers upon the wood
when Nesbit first came to London were John
Thurston, originally a copperplate engraver, and
William Marshall Craig, a miniature painter,
water-colour painter, and artistic jack-of-all-trades.
The former drew with exceptional skill, and
thoroughly understood the requirements of his
material; the latter, who designated himself "draw-

ing-master to the Princess Charlotte of Wales,"
and in 1821 had acquired sufficient position to
lecture before the "Royal Institution," was a
person of greatly inferior abilities. From the fact
that "Nesbit, sc." is to be found as early as 1800
upon the frontispiece of an edition of Bloomfield's
"Farmer's Boy," published by Vernor and Hood,
it is clear that he must have been employed almost
immediately upon the work of Thurston, by whom
this particular illustration was designed; and his
(Nesbit's) name is also included among the other
engravers engaged by Craig for the commonplace
"Scripture Illustrated" issued in 1806. Many
of the cuts to Wallis and Scholey's "History of
England" also bear Nesbit's signature. But his
best work about this date is to be found in the
"Religious Emblems" published by Ackermann
in 1809. This, according to the preface, was intended by its projector "to draw into one focus
all the talent of the day"; and, as a landmark in
the history of wood-engraving in England, its
position is a conspicuous one. The designs—and
the fact is significant after the foregoing announce-

THE CALL TO VIGILANCE.   *To face page* 178.

(ENGRAVED BY CLENNELL FOR ACKERMANN'S "RELIGIOUS EMBLEMS," 1809.)

ment—were without exception supplied by Thurston.[1] Regarded from an art point of view, and as designs alone, it is impossible to praise these very highly. Compared with Adrian van der Venne's illustrations to the emblems of Jacob Cats, or even with the efforts of the late C. H. Bennett, they show a poverty of invention which at times is almost beggarly. The " Destruction of Death and Sin " is typified by two prostrate figures at the foot of a cross ; " Fertilising Rills " is a landscape that might stand for anything; " Fainting for the Living Waters " is a limp female figure hanging Mazeppa-like upon a wounded stag; and Death felling trees is the only thing which the artist could think of to symbolise pictorially the common fate of humanity. These, however, are the least successful plates, and, setting imagination aside, they are nearly all distinguished by skill in composition and the arrangement of light and shade. Besides those by Nesbit, the cuts are

[1] So says the title-page. But there is a water-colour of an " allegorical subject," by Henry Tresham, R.A., at South Kensington, which strangely resembles Thurston's " Sinners hiding in the Grave." Tresham died in 1814.

engraved by Branston, Clennell, and Hole,—the last two being also pupils of Bewick. Hole's solitary "Seed Sown" is one of the best pieces of work in the book. Clennell and Branston are about equal in merit, but the honours belong to Nesbit. His "Hope Departing," "Joyful Retribution," and "Sinners Hiding in the Grave," the first especially, are almost faultless examples of patient and accomplished execution. "The World Weighed," the "Daughters of Jerusalem," and "Wounded in the Mental Eye," are nearly as good ; but as compositions they are less attractive than the others, and do not offer the same opportunities for the skilful opposition of black and white which seems specially to characterise Nesbit's manner. Yet, all things considered, they afford better examples of his abilities than either the large cut of "Rinaldo and Armida," or the illustrations—gems as some of them are—to Northcote's "Fables."

The "Rinaldo and Armida" is Nesbit's most ambitious block. It was engraved in 1818 for the "Practical Hints on Decorative Printing"

THE DAUGHTERS OF JERUSALEM.   *To face page* 180.

(ENGRAVED BY NESBIT FOR ACKERMANN'S "RELIGIOUS EMBLEMS," 1809.)

of William Savage, the printer, which, after long
delays, was published in 1822.   One feature of the
book was to have been four highly-finished plates
by the most eminent wood-engravers of the day.
But Bewick (whose name appears on the list of
subscribers) was too busy with "Æsop's Fables"
to give any assistance ; Clennell, who was to have
engraved a drawing by Stothard, had already
broken down ; and Branston and Nesbit were
the only contributors.   They engraved three of
Thurston's designs. Branston's subject, from Book
I. of the "Faerie Queen," was the "Cave of
Despair," which ranks as one of the artist's most
successful conceptions. Nesbit's were the "Female
and Boy," of which an electrotype is given at page
69 of Linton's "Hints on Wood-Engraving," and
"Rinaldo and Armida" in the enchanted garden,
from the "Gerusalemme Liberata" of Tasso. As
far as the execution of the background and accessories of the latter is concerned, we doubt if they
could be excelled, even at this day; but the figures
have a "dotted appearance," resulting from the
fact that Thurston required the engraver to reduce

the strength of the lines, which were "originally
continuous and distinct." Apart from this, however, the knight and enchantress are poorly and
even unpleasantly conceived. The "soft breast"
of Armida, which recurs so often in the fine old
translation of Fairfax, has the hardness and polish
of metal; while the figure of Rinaldo is marked
by a reposeless and over-accented muscularity,
which seems to have been one of Thurston's
besetting sins. To give rarity to this block, it
was defaced by criss-cross saw-marks, and impressions taken after it had been so treated are given
in Savage's book as an evidence of good faith.
As might have been predicted, the block was later
carefully repaired, and copies of it are still to be
found in the market as "original impressions."
Such a one (bought, alas! in too confiding a
moment) lies now before us; and it must be
admitted that the traces of the merciless steel
have been filled in with remarkable ingenuity,
although they are easily detected by an instructed
eye.

The "Rinaldo and Armida" must have been

executed during Nesbit's seclusion at Swalwell.
Besides the likeness of Bewick after Nicholson,
prefixed to Charnley's "Select Fables," the
only other works of importance that belong to
this date are those he contributed to the first

IN THE STOCKS.   (ENGRAVED BY NESBIT FOR BUTLER'S "HUDIBRAS," 1811.)

series of Northcote's "Fables," a book to which
we shall return more at length in speaking of
Harvey.   The best of these is the "Self-Important."   After his return to London, in 1830,
he was employed upon the second series, which
contains some of his most finished workmanship.
The cut of the "Hare and the Bramble," p. 127,

is one of the most beautiful of modern wood-
engravings.   In addition to the above-mentioned
books, he also engraved illustrations for "Shakespeare,"   "Hudibras,"   Somervile's   "Chase,"

THE SELF-IMPORTANT.   (ENGRAVED BY NESBIT FOR NORTHCOTE'S "FABLES," 1828.)

Stevens' "Lecture on Heads," and the numerous
reprints of Sir Egerton Brydges.   His cut to the
memory of Robert Johnson, after Johnson's own
design, is also much sought after by collectors.

Nesbit's fifteen years' absence from activity,

and the relatively small number of his productions, make the record of his life of the briefest;
and—as must be confessed—we have not been
able, after considerable pains, to add largely to
the facts already collected respecting him.   But

THE COCK, THE DOG, AND THE FOX.   (ENGRAVED BY NESBIT FOR
NORTHCOTE'S "FABLES," 1833.)

the excellence of his work as a wood-engraver
will always demand a record in the story of the
revival of the art.   In this respect he was the
best of Bewick's pupils, and his achievement was
in all probability greater than that of his fellows,
because he was not tempted beyond the limits of
his craft.

CHAPTER XI.

LUKE CLENNELL.

THE surname of Bewick's next pupil is a familiar
one to Northumbrians. There is, in fact, a
manor of Clennell on the east side of the river
Alwine, not far from Alwinton; and there was
even an actual Luke Clennell of that ilk who was
high-sheriff of Northumberland in 1727. Whether
the present Luke Clennell was in any way related
to this family has not been chronicled. He was
born at Ulgham, near Morpeth, on the 8th of
April 1781, being the son of a respectable farmer.
After covering his slate with sketches instead
of sums, an incident so persistently repeated in
artistic biography that it seems to be an almost
indispensable preliminary to distinction, he began
life, like Chodowiecki, as a grocer, or, as others

say, a tanner.   Here, if tradition is to be believed,
he got into trouble, owing to an ill-timed likeness
of an unsympathetic customer rashly depicted *ad
vivum* upon a convenient shop-door ; and some of
his other drawings having attracted attention, his
uncle, Thomas Clennell, of Morpeth, placed him
with Bewick.   This was in April 1797.   With
Bewick he remained seven years, and during his
apprenticeship is said to have transferred to the
block, and afterward engraved, a number of
Robert Johnson's designs, which were used as
tailpieces for the second volume of the "Birds."
He speedily became an expert draughtsman and
sketcher, and, like his master, was accustomed
to make frequent excursions into the country in
search of nature and the picturesque.   His term
of apprenticeship must have expired in April
1804 ; and, either shortly before this date or
immediately after it, he executed a number of
cuts for the "Hive of Ancient and Modern
Literature," a selection of essays, allegories, and
"instructive Compositions" in the "Blossoms of
Morality" manner, made by Solomon Hodgson,

Bewick's old partner in the "Quadrupeds." The third edition of this was published in 1806, and, according to Hugo, contains fourteen cuts by Bewick. This would give the majority of the illustrations to Clennell, who presumably designed as well as engraved them. That to the first part of the "Story of Melissa," a pretty little cut, bears his initials, and they are to be found on the "Northumberland Lifeboat." Some of the remaining cuts are also signed, and many of the rest may be confidently attributed to him; but those above mentioned are among the best.

Besides the engravings for the "Hive," he continued, after his apprenticeship was concluded, to work for Bewick on the illustrations to Wallis and Scholey's "History of England," already referred to in our account of Nesbit. Finding, however, that Bewick received the greater part of the money, he put himself into direct communication with the proprietors, the result being that they invited him to London, where he arrived in the autumn of 1804; and one of the earliest indications of his residence in the Metropolis is his

SHIP IN A GALE.

(Engraved by Clennell for Falconer's "Shipwreck," 1808.)

To face page 189.

receipt, in May 1806, of the "gold palette" of the
Society of Arts for "an engraving on wood of a
Battle." Among other books upon which he was
engaged were Craig's "Scripture Illustrated" and
Beattie's "Minstrel," 1807, from the designs of the
indispensable Thurston. Another volume belonging to this period was Falconer's "Shipwreck,"
1808, which contains a well-known picture of a
ship in a gale of wind, the manner of which is of
itself almost sufficient to prove his authorship of
some of the marine tailpieces in vol. ii. of the
"Birds." This cut was executed at Twickenham
in September 1807, and was much improved by
Clennell in the engraving. In 1809 appeared the
"Religious Emblems," of which we have already
given a sufficient description. Clennell's best
cuts in this are the "Call to Vigilance" and the
"Soul Encaged," but the least successful of the
series are also engraved by him.

Some time after his arrival in London, Clennell
married; the exact date is not known. His wife
was the eldest daughter of Charles Warren, the
copperplate engraver, a worthy rival of Abraham

Raimbach, Finden, and the little knot of talented
men who, at the beginning of the present century,
emulated each other in producing the delicate book-
embellishments issued by Sharpe, Du Rovery, and
others.   Clennell's introduction to this society
had, no doubt, an important influence over his
future career.   After Ackermann's " Emblems,"
his next work of importance was a large block for
the diploma of the Highland Society.   For this,
in 1809, he received the gold medal of the Society
of Arts.   Benjamin West made the design, which
consists of a circular frame containing an allegorical group, and flanked by two larger figures of
a fisherman and a Highland soldier.   Thurston
copied the figures within the frame on the wood ;
Clennell himself drew the supporters.   After he
had worked upon it for a couple of months, the
block, which was of box veneered upon beech, had
the same fate that befell the " Chillingham Bull " ;
it split, but irremediably, and history relates that
the chagrined artist, in a fit of disgust, flung the
tea-things into the fire.   In a few days, however,
he procured a fresh block, induced Thurston to

redraw the figures, and this time successfully completed his work, an example of which may be seen
in the collection of woodcuts at the South Ken-

DIPLOMA OF THE HIGHLAND SOCIETY.   (REDUCED FROM
CLENNELL'S CUT.)

sington Museum.[1]   It is thoroughly characteristic
of his style—a style rather energetic than fine, and
more spirited than minutely patient.   Fortune (it
should be added) was once more unfavourable to

[1] The bequest of John Thompson, the engraver.

the block, which was burnt in a fire at Bensley's printing-office; but the subject was subsequently engraved by John Thompson.

Clennell's last work of any moment as a wood-engraver is the series of cuts which illustrate Rogers's "Pleasures of Memory, with Other

HEADPIECE BY CLENNELL AFTER STOTHARD. (FROM ROGERS'S " PLEASURES OF MEMORY," 1810.)

Poems." This is usually dated 1812; but the copy before us, which has Clennell's name as engraver upon its title-page, bears the imprint of 1810. This little volume has an established reputation with collectors, and the excellence of the cuts as enlightened renderings of pen-and-ink sketches can scarcely be exaggerated. The touch

and spirit of the originals is given with rare fidelity, thoroughly to appreciate which it is only
necessary to contrast them with some of the later
copies in the modern editions of Rogers.   Many
of the compositions have all the lucid charm of
antique gems, and, indeed, may actually have been
copies of them, since the " Marriage of Cupid and
Psyche," p. 140, is plainly intended for the famous
sardonyx in the Marlborough collection.

Toward 1809 or 1810, and probably owing to
the enlarged views of art acquired in his father-in-
law's circle, Clennell seems virtually to have relin-
quished engraving for painting and designing.   He
had, in all likelihood, been preluding in this latter
direction for some time, as there is an engraving by Mantin in the British Museum after one of
his designs which dates as far back as 1803, and
he made many of the sketches for Scott's " Border
Antiquities."   In the Kensington Museum there
is, besides other sketches, a water-colour drawing
called the " Sawpit," dated 1810, which was shown
at the Exhibition of 1862 ; and in the Art Library
of the same institution there is a highly interesting

volume containing thirty compositions in water-colour, of which the majority were prepared for a series of "British Novelists," published by Sher-wood, Neely, and Jones in 1810-11. Many of these lightly-washed, slightly-worked sketches have a freedom and certainty of handling which were not retained when they were transferred to the copper, while the situations selected are often realised with considerable insight. It is true that they have not the grace of Stothard, but they have greater vigour. Clennell's men and women are a "strong generation":—in his hands Tom Jones becomes a broad-shouldered north-country fox-hunter, and Pickle's Emilia a bouncing Tyneside lass. But his designs have at least one advantage, the lack of which is a common charge against most modern book-illustra-tion,—they generally tell a story of some kind. "Trim in the Kitchen after Master Bobby's Death," from "Tristram Shandy," a subject which has exercised almost as many interpreters with the pencil as "Donec gratus eram" has found translators, is freshly treated, and can scarcely be said to fall much behind Stothard. This book of sketches contains some other drawings,—notably, a spirited one of a bull-baiting, and a few biographical particulars of which we shall hereafter make use.

In 1812 Clennell was living at 9 Constitution Row, Gray's Inn Lane Road, and he exhibited at the Royal Academy a lively picture of " Fox-hunters Regaling after the Pleasures of the Chase," which was engraved by his father-in-law, and later, in mezzotint, by T. Lupton. From this time forth he continued to exhibit drawings and paintings at the Academy, the British Institution, and the Exhibition of Painters in Water-Colours at the " Great Room, Spring Gardens," to which last he sent the largest number of contributions. The " Baggage Waggons in a Thunderstorm," exhibited in 1816 at the first-named place, and " The Day after the Fair," exhibited in 1818 at the British Institution, are characteristic examples of his work. Among the pictures which he sent to the water-colour gallery were several clever marine subjects, some fishing scenes especially.

One of these, the "Arrival of the Mackarel-
Boat," is held to be among his best productions.
A few of his sketches, the property of a New-
castle collector, Mr. Joseph Crawhall, were ex-
hibited at the Arts Association of that town in
October 1878. Others have been shown at the
Grosvenor Gallery and elsewhere.

But there are two pictures, not included in the
above list, which have special interest in the story
of Clennell's career : one was his masterpiece as
a painter, and the other has a tragic connection
with the terrible misfortune of his later years.
In March 1815 the British Institution set apart
1000 guineas to be awarded in premiums for
finished sketches in oil of subjects illustrating
the British successes under Wellington. Clennell
gained one of these premiums with a contribution,[1]
full of fire and furious movement, representing
the decisive charge at Waterloo. This was exhibited at the British Institution in 1816. The
remaining picture, the "Banquet of the Allied

[1] Now in the possession of Mrs. Vaughan, No. 88 Westbourne
Terrace.

Sovereigns in the Guildhall," was a commission
from the Earl of Bridgewater.   When Clennell
set to work upon this,—which it must be assumed
he did after he had completed the aforementioned
charge,—having grouped and lighted his composition, he took apartments in the west end of the
town (his latest residence appears to have been
in Pentonville), and waited patiently for the distinguished sitters who were to grace his board.
But in this part of his task he experienced so
much vexation, suspense, and fatigue, that, by the
time he had obtained the necessary sketches and
had commenced the picture in earnest, his intel-
lectual powers, probably already strained to their
utmost by his previous efforts, seem to have
suddenly given way.   This must have been early
in 1817.   The following account of the first indications of his malady, as related by one of his
friends, is contained in a letter to Mr. Chatto,
first published by him in his " History and Art of
Wood-Engraving," 1848, p. 22 :—

　　" I regret to say I was the cause of the first
discovery of his mind being affected. . . . I was

on very friendly terms with the family of his father-in-law, Charles Warren, the engraver—as fine a hearted man as ever breathed. I was consequently well acquainted with Clennell, and frequently visited him at his house in Pentonville. I have sat for hours beside him whilst he was engaged in painting that fatal picture. One night, a large party of young folks had assembled at Mr. Warren's,—a very frequent occurrence, for everybody went there when they wished to be happy; and we had spent a long night in junketting and play, and games of all sorts, twirling the trencher, being, as I well remember, one of them; and at last had gathered in a large circle round the fire. Clennell was seated next the fire on one side, and I sat next to him. I had remarked that for at least half-an-hour before he had been looking vacantly under the grate, paying no attention to the fun that was going on. In order to rouse him, I gave him a hearty slap on the thigh, and said: 'Why, Clennell, you are in a brown study!' He gave a faint laugh and said, 'Indeed, I think I am.' He did not, however,

become so much roused as to pay any attention
to the *mêlée* of waggery that was going on.   We
broke up about one o'clock ; and on my calling at
Mr. Warren's next afternoon, I was shocked to
hear from him that he feared Clennell's mind was
affected ; for that about three in the morning,
after having gone home with his wife and retired
to bed, he started up and dressed himself, telling
his wife that he was going to her father's on a
very important affair.   As his wife could not pre-
vail on him to defer his visit to a more seasonable
hour, she determined to accompany him.   On
arriving at Gray's Inn Road, he knocked violently;
and on being let in by Mr. Warren, he said that
he had been grossly insulted by *me*, and that he
was determined on having immediate satisfaction.
All Mr. Warren's arguments as to the impossi-
bility of my having intended to insult him were
met with positive assertions to the contrary.   He
said that he knew better; ' I had been placed
next him on purpose, and it was a preconcerted
thing.'   Mr. Warren at last, seeing how it was
with him, humoured him so far as to say that he

would go with him, and have an explanation, an
apology, *or* satisfaction! They accordingly set
out for my house; but Mr. Warren, being now
quite sensible on the subject, instead of proceeding toward my house, took a very different direction, and led him about till he became tired: he
was at that time anything but strong. He also
by degrees quieted his mind towards me, by
speaking of my friendship for him and my love of
art; and by daylight he got him home and to
bed. I need hardly say what exquisite pain this
account gave me, for I really loved Clennell: he
was always so mild, so amiable—in short, such a
GOOD fellow."

Shortly after this, becoming mischievous, Clennell was placed in an asylum in London. Under
the pressure of misfortune, his wife's mind also
gave way, and she died, leaving three children.
By the exertions of Sir John Swinburne (grandfather of the poet) and other benevolent persons,
the Waterloo charge was engraved, in 1819, by
W. Bromley. It was published by the Committee
of the Artists' Fund, to which institution Clennell

had belonged, and the proceeds were vested in trustees for the benefit of himself and his family. The same body, says Pye, protected him to the day of his death, which took place in February 1840.

During the long period which intervened between 1817 and 1840, Clennell never wholly recovered, though hopes appear to have been entertained that his reason might be restored. For some years he remained in London, but he was subsequently transferred to the care of his relations in the North. When Mackenzie wrote his "History of Newcastle," in 1827, he was living in this way at Tritlington ; later, he was at St. Peter's Quay. Once he called upon Bewick and asked him for a block to engrave, but when, to humour him, he had been supplied with one, his efforts resembled those of an unskilled first beginner. His faculty for drawing appears to have less declined. We have now before us a bullfinch and a group of carnations,[1] which he is stated to

[1] For access to these, and the verses hereafter printed, we are indebted to the kindness of Mr. W. B. Scott, the painter and poet, some of whose earlier years were spent in Newcastle, the Literary and Philosophical Society of which is embellished by

have executed during his insanity; and, except
that they are slightly exaggerated in size, the
handling is unfaltering and effective. In his
earlier days he had been acquainted with Burns,
whose songs he sang; and one of the amusements
of his vacant hours consisted in composing strange
and half-articulate fragments of verse, a few specimens of which are reproduced in the "History of
Wood-Engraving." In the "Athenæum" for
7th March 1840, there are three more,—"Sole-
man," "A Floweret," and "The Lady upon her
Palfrey Grey,"—and others have been published
elsewhere. The following, which, as far as can be
ascertained, have not appeared in any type save
that of the rare leaflet on which they were first
printed, are here given chiefly for that reason, and
not for any special merit they possess as poetry :

---

one of his pictures, "The Building of the new Castle by the son
of William the Conqueror." To his many artistic tastes Mr.
Scott adds a love of Bewick, and he cherishes as a memento,
mounted in a cane-head, the original button engraved by Bewick
as a model for the "Northumberland Hunt." It bears a running
fox, and is inscribed "Engraved by T. Bewick. Given by him to
W. Losh, Esq."

A BALLAD.

THE hill it was high
    As the maiden did climb,
And O she wished for her true love nigh,
    And dearly she wished for the time
That she might be by
Her own true love of the azure sky.
The hill it was fair,
And sweet was the air,
    But her true love was not nigh ;
The cowslips look gay,
Her love is on his way,
    And they meet on the hill of the sky.

AN EPIC UPON WINTER.

IN January or November's cold,
When stern winter his sceptre doth hold
By farm, or common side, or village lane,
Or where the sturdy peasant
Doth drive a drain,

Cutting his way
Oft through the frozen clay ;
Sometimes dressing a hedge,
Lopping away the cumbrous sedge—
There the fendifair, in numerous wing,
To taste, now fresh, the oozing spring,
And flock in the copse or on the bough,
In winter's merriment to dow.
Perhaps, near a gravel-pit,
Where doth the swiller boy
To carry sand his time employ,
The little sandybird doth sit
Upon a twig,
In expectation big—
Or robin or blackbird in haste
The new brown atom to taste,
And pick their welcome cheer,
In winter's month so often drear.

To attach any undue importance to these irregular verses would be absurd ; but the inborn love of nature is still discernible in the disjointed imagery and the poor rudderless words. Both pieces bear the author's initials, " L. C.," and are dated from " St. Peters."

While at St. Peters, Clennell appears to have been harmless ; but in 1831 he again became unmanageable, and was placed in an asylum, where he remained until he died. In 1844 a monumental tablet by R. Davies, a local sculptor, was erected to his memory in St. Andrew's Church, Newcastle.

It is difficult to determine the precise limits of talents so fatally interrupted, or to decide definitely whether their possessor should or should not be included among "the inheritors of unfulfilled renown." When attacked by his malady he was six-and-thirty, and if there be any truth in the axiom of Joseph de Maistre that "he who has not conquered at thirty will never conquer," Clennell had already passed that critical stage. But we do not place much faith in the utterance in question, and, setting speculation aside, it may fairly be affirmed of him that he was, after Nesbit, the best engraver among Bewick's pupils; and that when his mind gave way he was beginning to show powers of a higher kind as an artist, particularly in the line of landscape and rustic scenes. His distinguishing qualities are breadth, spirit, and rapidity of handling, rather than finish and minuteness; and the former characteristics are usually held to be superior to the latter. His unfortunate story invests them with an additional interest.

CHAPTER XII.

HARVEY, JACKSON, ETC.

WILLIAM HARVEY, the third of Bewick's pupils
who attained to any distinction, is known chiefly
as a designer on wood, and for a considerable
period held the foremost place in the profession.
In these days, when artists of this class are so
numerous, it is difficult to understand how one man
could completely command the field ; and yet it
seems certain that, about 1830-40, Harvey was
the sole person to whom engravers could apply
for an original design with security, and who devoted himself exclusively to the preparation of
such designs. "The history of wood-engraving,"
says a writer in the "Art Union" for 1839, "for
some years past, is almost a record of the works
of his (Harvey's) pencil." It was the custom to

PART OF HAYDON'S "DENTATUS."
(FROM HARVEY'S ENGRAVING, 1821.)

To face page 207.

say that he produced more than Stothard or Chodowiecki; but it would be more appropriate to
compare his unflagging fertility to that of Doré or
Gilbert. He was born at Westgate, 13th July
1796, his father being keeper of the Newcastle
Baths. At fourteen he was apprenticed to
Bewick, with whom he became a great favourite,
as may be gathered from the well-nigh par-
ental letter, printed in Chatto's Treatise, which
Bewick addressed to him in 1815. Harvey
worked with Temple, another pupil, upon the
"Fables" of 1818, and, it is alleged, transferred
many of Johnson's sketches to the wood. In
September 1817 he removed to London. Here
he studied drawing under B. R. Haydon, and
anatomy under Sir Charles Bell. While with
Haydon (where he had Eastlake, Lance, and
Landseer for fellow-pupils), he engraved the
well-known block after Haydon's "Assassination
of Dentatus"—that ambitious attempt to unite
colour, expression, handling, light, shadow, and
heroic form, of which, if report is to be believed,
the proximate destination was a packing-case in

Lord Mulgrave's stable. Harvey's engraving has
been described as "probably the largest, certainly
the most laboured, block that had then been cut
in England"; but its manifest and misguided
rivalry of copperplate makes it impossible to
praise it as highly as its exceedingly skilful technique would seem to warrant. As a work upon

INITIAL LETTERS BY HARVEY. (FROM HENDERSON'S "HISTORY OF WINES," 1824.)

wood it must be regarded as more ingenious than
admirable.

Towards 1824 Harvey seems wholly to have
abandoned engraving for design, his decision in
this direction being apparently determined by the
success of the illustrations he drew and in part cut
for Henderson's "History of Ancient and Modern
Wines." These are some of his most pleasing per-

HEADPIECE.

(DRAWN AND ENGRAVED BY HARVEY FOR HENDERSON'S "HISTORY OF WINES," 1824.)

To face page 208.

formances.   As engravings they are excellent ; as
compositions they have but little of the unpleasant
mannerism which afterward grew upon him and
disfigured his later work.   To give an account of

THE EGRET.   (FROM A DRAWING BY HARVEY.)

his labours as a designer subsequent to this time
would be unnecessary as well as tedious.   About
1830 he had become prominently popular in this
way ; he was at the height of his reputation in
1840, and when he died, six-and-twenty years

later, his work was still in request. His designs
for the " Tower Menagerie," 1828; "Zoological
Gardens," 1830-31; " Children in the Wood,"
1831; " Blind Beggar of Bethnal Green," 1832;
" Story without an End," " Pictorial Prayer Book,"

THE JAGUAR.　(DRAWN BY HARVEY FOR " THE TOWER MENAGERIE," 1828.)

" Bible," " Shakspere,"[1] and a hundred other
issues from Charles Knight's untiring press, attest
his industry and versatility. Those who desire
to study him to advantage, however, will do so in

[1] Bogue's Bunyan's " Pilgrim's Progress," engraved by the
Dalziels, is also one of Harvey's better efforts.

MAAROOF BIDDING FAREWELL TO HIS WIFE.

(Drawn by Harvey for Lane's "Thousand and One Nights," 1840.)

To face page 211.

the two series of Northcote's "Fables," 1828 and
1833, to which we have already referred ; and in
Lane's "Thousand and One Nights," 1838-40.
Northcote, indeed, takes credit for the illustrations
in the former case ; but from the accounts which
exist of the way in which he prepared the merely
indicatory sketches that Harvey subsequently elaborated and transferred to the block,[1] and from
the admission in the preface to vol. i. that many
of the designs have been " improved by his

[1] " It was by a curious process that Mr. Northcote really
made the designs for those Fables the amusement of his old age,
for his talents as a draftsman, excelling as he did in Animals, was
rarely required by this undertaking.   His general practice was to
collect great numbers of prints of animals, and to cut them out ;
he then moved such as he selected about upon the surface of a
piece of paper until he had illustrated the fable by placing them
to his satisfaction, and had thus composed his subject, then fixing
the different figures with paste to the paper, a few pen or pencil
touches rendered this singular composition complete enough to
place in the hands of Mr. Harvey, by whom it was adapted or
freely translated on the blocks for the engravers.   The designs
made by this ingenious mode are the more curious as having been
executed by a painter, whose masterly hand knew so well how to
give that beauty of arrangement which makes them so admirable
and interesting."—" Sketch of the Life of James Northcote, Esq.,
R.A.," by E. S. Rogers, prefixed to the second series of " Fables,"
1833.

(Harvey's) skill," it is probable that most of the honours of the undertaking really belong to Harvey, though he again, no doubt, profited in some degree by having Northcote's first ideas to

THE GREAT EAGLE-OWL. (DRAWN BY HARVEY FOR " THE GARDENS AND THE MENAGERIE OF THE ZOOLOGICAL SOCIETY," 1831.)

energise upon. The ornamental letters and vignettes were entirely his own. Taken as a whole, these two volumes are among the most interesting examples of woodcut art in England. They were a labour of love to their projector, whose dying regret

GARDENS ON THE RIVER OF EL-UBULLEH. *To face page* 213.
(DRAWN BY HARVEY FOR LANE'S "THOUSAND AND ONE NIGHTS," 1840.)

it was that he had not lived to see the publication
of the second series; and some of the happiest
work of Nesbit, Jackson, Thompson, and Williams
—that is to say, of the most successful wood-engravers of the day—is to be found in their pages.

PARTY QUARRELS.   (ENGRAVED BY JACKSON FOR NORTHCOTE'S
"FABLES," 1833.)

In the "Arabian Nights," which is regarded
as Harvey's masterpiece, he is free from any
charges of collaboration, beyond the fact that he
worked under the eye of Mr. Lane, who assisted
him with minute indications of costume and accessories.   In the life of Lane by his nephew,

Mr. Stanley Lane-Poole, it is stated that the
former did not attach much importance to these
pictorial embellishments, and even thought that
they might well be dispensed with.   Some allow-
ance must be made in this case for Mr. Lane's
unique position as a critic.   A Roman of the
time of Augustus would doubtless find anachron-
isms in the works of Gérôme ; and no designer
would have been likely to entirely satisfy the in-
veterate Egyptologist, who had himself sat cross-
legged in the ancient Arab city of Cairo, and who,
to the end of his life, began each day's task with a
pious *Bismi-lláh*.   That Lane's disciple, relative,
and biographer should, under the circumstances,
speak of Harvey's drawings as the " least excellent
part of the book," and damn them with the faint
praise of "succeeding in some slight degree in
catching the oriental spirit of the tales," is perhaps
to be anticipated ; but the fact remains that the
artist reached his highest point in these volumes,
and the public of Charles Knight's time probably
ranked them far above the text in importance.
A certain florid and luxuriant facility, which in

THE SECOND SHEYKH RECEIVING HIS POOR BROTHER.
(Drawn by Harvey for Lane's "Thousand and One Nights," 1840.)

To face page 215.

Harvey's ordinary designs is monotonous or ill-timed, seems almost in keeping with Eastern subjects, and many of the headpieces and vignettes, set tastefully in intricate arabesques, and beautifully engraved by Jackson and his colleagues, are gems of refined and delicate invention. Speaking generally, the decorative and topographical examples, the glimpses of bazaar and street, of mosque and turreted gate and "latticed meshrebeeyeh," are superior to the picturesquely grouped but expressionless figure subjects. In drawing animals, Harvey was often singularly fortunate, although here, as always, his peculiar mannerism mars his work.

At his death, in 1866, he was Bewick's only surviving pupil. Beyond the fact that he was a thoroughly amiable and unpretentious man, and an unwearied worker, little of interest has been recorded respecting him. A new race of draughtsmen has sprung up since he laid down the pencil, but his name will always deserve to be remembered in the annals of his craft. He lies buried in the cemetery at Richmond.

In addition to the pupils already mentioned, there were a few others, who either did not attain to celebrity, or whose relationship to Bewick was of a more incidental kind. Foremost among these comes John Jackson, who was born at Ovingham in 1801, and died in 1848. Redgrave says that he was a pupil of Armstrong (which is indefinite), and afterwards of Bewick. With the latter he had some obscure disagreement which prematurely terminated their connection, Bewick, it is alleged, going even so far as to cut his own and his son's names out of the unexpired indentures. Jackson then moved to London, and worked for a time under Harvey, many of whose designs he subsequently engraved. He either did, or superintended, much of the work on the " Penny Magazine" and other of Charles Knight's various enterprises ; and between 1830 and 1840 was the busiest and best employed of London wood-engravers.[1] His work for the two series of North-

[1] Many good examples of Jackson's work are to be found in a volume of 150 selected engravings from the " Penny Magazine," published in 1835, and referred to before a Committee of the

cote's " Fables " and Lane's " Arabian Nights "
has already been mentioned.   As an engraver he
was careful and painstaking without any special
show of genius.   His name has, however, acquired

THE FOX, THE WEASEL, AND THE RABBIT.   (ENGRAVED BY JACKSON
FOR NORTHCOTE'S " FABLES," 1828.)

more prominence than it perhaps actually deserves, from its connection with a book to
which we have frequently made reference, and

House of Commons as illustrating the progress and advantages
of popular woodcut art.

to which no student of wood-engraving can fail
to be indebted, namely, the "Treatise" on that
art, hitherto currently known as "Jackson and
Chatto." When this volume first appeared in 1839,

THE WOODCOCK.   (ENGRAVED BY JACKSON AFTER BEWICK'S CUT.)

an angry controversy arose as to the relative claims
of the engraver and his colleague to the honours of
authorship.   We do not propose to stir the ashes
of this ancient dispute.   Still, it may be stated
that Mr. Chatto appears to have had but scant
justice done to him in the matter, for, with a few

reservations, the composition and preparation of
the book were entirely his.   Indeed, Jackson was
in no sense "literary," and could not possibly
have undertaken it ; and although he provided
and paid for the illustrations, the attributing of
them *en masse* to him personally is manifestly an

THE PARTRIDGE.   (ENGRAVED BY JACKSON AFTER BEWICK'S CUT.)

error, as the major part of the facsimiles of old
woodcuts were the work of the late Mr. Fairholt,
and were chiefly engraved by a young pupil of
Jackson's named Stephen Rimbault.   Others were
executed by J. W. Whymper.   Of the blocks
actually from the graver of Jackson himself, the
best are the " Partridge " and the " Woodcock "

after Bewick, which are favourable specimens of his powers. Jackson's true position with regard to the whole book seems to have been rather that of projector than of author; and it is satisfactory to know that in the third edition, which has been

THE VAIN BUTTERFLY. (ENGRAVED BY LANDELLS FOR NORTHCOTE'S " FABLES," 1833.)

recently issued, due prominence has been given on the title-page to the hitherto insufficiently recognised labours of Mr. Chatto.

With the exception of Ebenezer Landells, the remaining pupils of Bewick are little more than names. Landells was an excellent engraver, who did good work on the " Illustrated London News "

'SEED SOWN.'

(ENGRAVED BY HOLE FOR ACKERMANN'S "RELIGIOUS EMBLEMS," 1809.)

To face page 221.

and " Punch," and succeeded admirably in rendering the animals of Thomas Landseer. He died
in 1860. Hole, already referred to in connection
with Ackermann's " Religious Emblems," and
whose full name was Henry Fulke Plantagenet
Woolicombe Hole, was the son of a captain in the
Lancashire militia. He practised as an engraver
at Liverpool, but ultimately gave up the profession
on succeeding to an estate in Devonshire. He
did some of the cuts in the " British Birds," and
a much-lauded vignette to Shepherd's " Poggio."
W. W. Temple, who assisted Harvey in " Bewick's
Fables" of 1818, became a draper at the end of
his apprenticeship. Henry White, who engraved
Thurston's designs to Burns, as well as many of
Cruikshank's squibs for Hone, and some of the
best of the cuts in Yarrell's " Fishes," was an exceedingly clever workman. Of John Johnson,
Robert Johnson's cousin, who designed the cut
of the " Hermit" in Goldsmith's and Parnell's
" Poems," we have no material particulars. Isaac
Nicholson, Anderson, Edward Willis, and the rest,
may be dismissed without further mention.

TAILPIECE. (FROM NORTHCOTE'S "FABLES," 1828.)

APPENDIX.

LIST of the oil-paintings, water-colour drawings, prints, etc., presented by the Executors of Miss Isabella Bewick to the Museum of the Natural History Society of Northumberland, Durham, and Newcastle-upon-Tyne, in March 1884 :—

Portrait of Thomas Bewick, by J. Ramsay, oil-painting.
   Do.   do.   T. S. Good, oil-painting.
   Do.   do.   Miss Kirkley.
   Do.   do.   Miniature by Murphy.
   Do.   do.   do.   by Plymer.
   Do. Miniature of Moses Griffith, friend of Tennant.
   Do. of John Bewick, by George Gray, crayon.
   Do. of Robert E. Bewick when a boy, by John Bell, oil-painting.

DRAWINGS.

12 Small coloured drawings of foreign birds, unmounted.

 1 Sketch of horse in crayons, by John Bewick.

89 Coloured drawings of Wycliffe birds, nearly all foreign, mounted on ten sheets, and numbered 1, 2, 3, 5, 7, 8, 9, 10, 11, 12.

12 Coloured drawings of birds, mounted on six sheets by Rev. C. Kingsley :—Roller, nutcracker, great spotted woodpecker, chough, red-backed shrike, cuckoo, bunting, ptarmigan, jackdaw, hooded crow, turtle-dove, and pied flycatcher.

2 Drawings, mounted by Ruskin, on one sheet :—Wren coloured, and vignette in pencil.

46 Drawings of water birds, mounted on four sheets, numbered 3, 5, 6, 7.

> Sheet 3. Olivaceous gallinule, water hen, head of razorbill, little grebe, great crested grebe, great auk, do. do., Sclavonian grebe, red-throated diver, black guillemot, great Northern diver (all coloured).

> Sheet 5. Goosander, merganser, smew, red-breasted goose, eider duck, brent goose, bean goose, eider duck (coloured) and goosander, wild swan, mute swan, do. do. (in pencil).

> Sheet 6. Wigeon, golden eye, sheldrake, cormorant, long-tailed duck, tufted duck, golden eye, garganey, gannet (coloured), pintail, and castaneous duck (in pencil).

> Sheet 7. Scoter (coloured) and cormorant (young), gannet, olivaceous gallinule, and eight portions of birds (in pencil).

35 Drawings mounted on nine sheets, A to I inclusive.

> Sheet A. Great plover, greenshank (coloured), and goshawk (in pencil).

> Sheet B. Crossbill (red plumage), whinchat, yellow wagtail (coloured), and little stint (in pencil).

Sheet C. Capercailzie, night heron, and two vignettes (coloured).

Sheet D. Foreign lark, green woodpecker, a spotted crake, nightingale (coloured).

Sheet E. Redwing, great black-backed gull (young), black-headed gull (immature), red-necked phalarope (coloured).

Sheet F. Reed fauvette, ash-coloured sandpiper, wryneck, snipe (coloured).

Sheet G. Dunlin, long-tailed tit, goldfinch (coloured), and jacana-like bird, and peacock (in pencil).

Sheet H. 4 Vignettes (coloured).

Sheet I. 3 Do. do.

68 Drawings in pencil, mounted on three sheets, numbered 10, 11, 12.

Sheet 10. Barnacle goose, spurwinged goose, gadwall, wild duck, brent goose, Egyptian goose, Muscovy duck, king duck, cravat goose, shoveler, white-fronted goose, scaup duck, garganey, Egyptian goose, harlequin duck, bimaculated duck.

Sheet 11. 23 Vignettes in pencil.

Sheet 12. 29 Do. do.

25 Sketches in pencil, mounted on three sheets of tinted paper, numbered 13, 14, 15.

Sheet 13 contains 9 sketches.

,, 14 ,, 8 do.

,, 15 ,, 8 do.

14 Slight sketches of animals in pencil.

10 Slight sketches of animals in pencil.

14 Drawings of birds in colours :—

> Great bittern, sparrow hawk, red-necked grebe, mag-
> pie, Pennant's parrot, pied wagtail, common fowl,
> waxwing, kestrel, golden plover, red phalarope,
> dipper, red-throated diver, nightjar.
> Drawing—Whitley ox.
> Slight pencil sketch, called Chillingham Bull.
> Pidcock's elephant in pencil.
> Sketch of sheep in pencil.
> Horse and groom in pencil.
> Whitley ox in Indian ink.
> Spotted hyena in pencil.

255 Slight drawings by Thomas, John, and Robert Bewick.
> A set of the cuts of the quadrupeds coloured by Bewick
> for his children, bound.

11 Engraved portraits of Thomas Bewick.

4 Vignettes in frame, water-colours.
> Man with leister, rock with stone monument, man and
> dog at park gates, men carrying large tub.

4 Do.　do.　Cottage in winter, wreck of boat lying on
> shore, monumental stone and figures, dog and hen
> and chickens.

Framed.　Pennant's short-eared owl, water-colour.
Do.　　Spearman's kyloe ox,　　　do.
Do.　　Ox grazing,　　　　　　do.
Do.　　Chillingham bull, proof on vellum, with border, in
　　　　first state.
Do.　　Trotting horse, lithographed by Thomas Bewick.
Do.　　Waiting for death, proof on vellum.
Do.　　Lion, done for Pidcock.

Framed. Elephant, done for Pidcock.

Do. Whitley ox, drawn and engraved on copper by
Thomas Bewick, 1789.

Do. Old horse, small copperplate, by T. Bewick.

Do. Huntsman and hound, woodcut.

Do. Ramsay's portrait of T. B., engraved by Burnet.

WOOD ENGRAVINGS.

Prints of quadrupeds, land and water birds, foreign birds,
British fishes, vignettes, prints for " Fables of Æsop,"
"Select Fables," etc., amounting to about 2445 examples.
Baily's bust of Bewick in plaster, and pedestal.

COMMON DUCK. (FROM BEWICK'S "THREE HUNDRED ANIMALS," 1819.)

TAILPIECE. (FROM NORTHCOTE'S "FABLES," 1828.)

INDEX.

[The dates given, with few exceptions, are those of the first editions.]

THE END.